YOUTH
UNDER CONSTRUCTION

BUILDING A
BIBLICAL
YOUTH MINISTRY

TIM HAWKINS
Foreword by Dr. Tom Sexton

Youth Under Construction

TIM HAWKINS

A ministry of **Gulf Coast Baptist Church**
Dr. Tom Sexton, Pastor
312 SE 24th Ave, Cape Coral, FL 33990
(239) 574-STAR   www.5scp.com

YOUTH UNDER CONSTRUCTION

Printed in the United States of America.

Printed by Faith Baptist Church Publications
Fort Pierce, Florida
www.fbcpublications.com

DEDICATION

My deepest gratitude is extended to those who have personally influenced my faith in Christ and philosophy in youth ministry.

Dr. Joel & Jackie Hawkins
My parents who have prayerfully raised three teenagers to honor and serve the Lord Jesus Christ.

Dr. Tom Sexton
My father-in-law and pastor of the Gulf Coast Baptist Church in Cape Coral, Florida, who constantly inspires me through his leadership, vision, and burden for souls.

Dr. Larry Brown
Pastor of the Victory Baptist Church of North Augusta, South Carolina, who exemplifies the joy of serving Jesus and the primacy of preaching.

Dr. Clarence Sexton

Pastor of the Temple Baptist Church in Powell, TN,
for personal training I received through the annual
Pastors College and School of Youth Ministries.

Dr. Steve Hurte

Associate pastor of the Victory Baptist Church of
North Augusta, South Carolina, and a true friend who
strengthened my hand in the Lord.

Dr. Michael Haynes

Pastor of the Trident Baptist Church of Goose Creek,
South Carolina, who impacted my life in
the teen years as my youth director.

Dr. Randy Rhye

Former pastor of the Sharon Baptist Church in
Cumming, Georgia, who along with his wife Phyllis,
guided Mandy and me early in our
marriage and ministry.

TABLE OF CONTENTS

SELECTING THE RIGHT BLUEPRINT

SURVEYING THE LAND

SUPERVISING THE PROJECT

SETTING THE FOUNDATION

STRENGTHENING THE WALLS

SHINGLING THE ROOF

SURVIVING THE FINAL INSPECTION

FOREWORD

Nothing encourages me more than to see young people grow up and have a heart for our Lord Jesus and His work.

Psalm 33:11 says, *"The counsel of the LORD standeth for ever, the thoughts of His heart to all generations."*

Brother Hawkins is my generation's next generation. I have witnessed his transformation from a teenager to a strong preacher of God's Word. He is now writing for his next generation.

The truths in this book have been used in our ministry over the last fifteen years to build and strengthen young people to become servants of our Lord Jesus.

I am thinking of so many young people who are serving the Lord out of our youth ministry. I know that one day we will rejoice at the Judgment Seat of Christ over what has been accomplished in their lives as they hold forth the Word of life.

I encourage every pastor and all who work with young people to use this book.

Dr. Tom Sexton, John 8:29

Acknowledgements

I want to express much thanks to the following people who made the publication of this book possible.

For typing: Lena Noble

For editing and proofreading: Jamie Womble

For cover design: Joy Manning

For quality printing: Faith Baptist Church Publications in Fort Pierce, Florida

For publishing: Five Star Christian Publications, a ministry of Gulf Coast Baptist Church in Cape Coral, Florida.

SELECTING THE RIGHT BLUEPRINT

When beginning a construction project, the most important stage is to acquire a blueprint from the architect. A wise builder will refer to these instructions over and over as he accomplishes the work of construction. This blueprint will help him in making right decisions. It will guide him in understanding the details. His overall measure of success will depend upon following these plans precisely. If he deviates from the blueprint, there will be much confusion over what is right and what is wrong, and the end result will not be acceptable.

When building a youth ministry for the glory of God, there is a wide range of opinion over what is the right way and what is the wrong way. God has not left the important task of constructing lives up to our own opinions and ideas. The Divine Architect of Heaven has given us a blueprint for building and developing the local church youth ministry. It is the Bible. God's Holy Word is inspired, inerrant, preserved, and relevant. It is the detailed blueprint needed to build a well-balanced youth ministry. Any program, idea, activity, or philosophy that leads us away from God's blueprint for the youth ministry is dangerous and destructive.

Today's youth minister will face much pressure to abandon the emphasis of God's Word. If he yields, he will suffer loss at the Judgment Seat of Christ. The local church youth ministry can make a lasting impact upon the lives of teenagers by adhering to God's blueprint in philosophy and practice.

CHAPTER 1

PUTTING THE BIBLE BACK INTO THE YOUTH MINISTRY

When working with teenagers, it will not be long until we are faced with a tragic realization: we have raised a generation of biblically illiterate young people. Most teenagers have never been taught even the most basic of Bible stories. There is no common ground on which we can relate to them spiritually because there has never been a biblical foundation laid in their hearts and minds.

A recent survey was taken by the Gallup Poll asking two thousand teenagers their views on religion and the Bible. Only 13% said they read the Bible often. Only 36% believe the Bible is the literal Word of God. 65% could not name four of the Ten Commandments. 68% could not name four of the twelve disciples.[1] No wonder Satan has devoured so many young lives in this generation. God's Word says, *"My people are destroyed for lack of knowledge..."* (Hosea 4:6).

> The true measure of a successful youth ministry is not determined by large numbers, but by our *loyalty* to the Word of God.

The true measure of a successful youth ministry is not determined by *large numbers*, but by our *loyalty* to the Word of God. The desire of every youth ministry should be to develop exemplary, Christian young people who have a heart for God. God's Word is the vehicle that will take us to this desired end. There will be no true success apart from the Scriptures. If we are to accomplish God's will in God's way, we must put the Bible back into the youth ministry.

Some teenagers believe the Bible is not relevant to their circumstances. Hence, some youth directors have minimized the teaching and preaching of the Bible, and they have maximized activities, sports, games, and recreation in an attempt to connect with young people. This "cookie and Kool-Ade" approach to the youth ministry will not build spiritual teenagers. Teens must be taught that the Bible is not "out of touch" with their generation. The youth minister must make a deliberate, purposeful attempt to rightly divide the Word of God and meet the teenager head-on with the issues they are facing in life. We must firmly believe that the answer is still scriptural, despite the world's cry of irrelevance.

In I Timothy 4:12-16, the apostle Paul instructed young Timothy to give attendance to the Word of God in his life and ministry. ***"Let no man despise thy youth;***

but be thou an example of the believers, in word, in conversation, in charity, in spirit, in faith, in purity. Till I come, give attendance to reading, to exhortation, to doctrine. Neglect not the gift that is in thee, which was given thee by prophecy, with the laying on of the hands of the presbytery. Meditate upon these things; give thyself wholly to them; that thy profiting may appear to all. Take heed unto thyself, and unto the doctrine; continue in them: for in doing this thou shalt both save thyself, and them that hear thee." This same Biblical pattern should be taught to and followed by teenagers in the local church youth ministry.

READ GOD'S WORD
"...give attendance to reading..."
I Timothy 4:13

Satan has finally found a way to keep God's people from believing the Bible. It is to keep them from reading it. The average Christian teenager has *dirt* in their heart and *dust* on their Bible. Many teenage failures could be avoided if we could get them to read the Bible on a daily basis. Isaiah 34:16 says, *"Seek ye out of the book of the LORD, and read: no one of these shall fail...."*

> The average Christian teenager has *dirt* in their heart and *dust* on their Bible.

G. Campbell Morgan said that the Bible can be read through in just 60 hours. It has been said that George Mueller (1805 – 1898) read through the Bible over 200 times in his life. Many people have never read it through in an entire lifetime.

We must seek to challenge young people to succeed in this area. This can be done by providing a daily, monthly, or yearly devotional guide that will walk them through God's Word in a systematic way and by encouraging them to be accountable to someone.

RECEIVE THE EXHORTATION OF GOD'S WORD
"...give attendance to...exhortation..."
I Timothy 4:13

Young people not only need to read the Bible for themselves, they also need to listen to the teaching and preaching of the Word of God. Very few young people know the doctrines of our faith. Doctrine has been replaced with humorous stories, current events, news clippings, and videos. Many teens are being indoctrinated with humanism, evolution, rock music, rap music, gang life and language, homosexuality, and violence.

Young people cannot be *"throughly furnished"* without the doctrine, reproof, correction, and instruction of the Word of God (II Timothy 3:16-17). Any program that separates the teenager from the preaching and teaching ministry of the pulpit should be abandoned. As youth leaders, we must seize every opportunity to place truth into the hearts of young people. It is important to keep them under the influence of the pulpit at every available church service: Sunday morning, Sunday evening, and Wednesday evening. When the exhortation of Scripture is *magnified,* the elevation of sin will be *minimized.*

> When the exhortation of Scripture is *magnified,* the elevation of sin will be *minimized.*

BUILD CONVICTIONS FROM GOD'S WORD
"...give attendance to...doctrine."
I Timothy 4:13

Our teenagers need to know what they believe and why they believe it. They need to be taught specific, biblical principles on which they can base their daily decisions, appearance, and conduct. We should not seek to make standards for them but rather teach them to make standards for themselves from God's Word, stressing obedience to Christ in every area of life. Failure in this area will produce *temporarily conformed* teens rather than *permanently transformed* teens.

This is a day for boldness in the lives of God's people. Immorality is often pushed and promoted in this generation, while Bible-believing Christians remain silent. When teenagers learn to develop personal convictions from the Bible, they will stand strong for the Lord Jesus Christ.

MEDITATE ON AND MEMORIZE GOD'S WORD

"Meditate upon these things; give thyself wholly to them; that thy profiting may appear to all."
I Timothy 4:15

There is a two-fold goal we should seek to accomplish in the lives of young people. One is to get teenagers into the Bible, the other is to get the Bible into teenagers. One is accomplished through reading the Scripture, the other is accomplished through meditating on and memorizing the Scripture. This will keep young people from sin. Psalm 119:11, *"Thy word have I hid in mine heart, that I might not sin against thee."* Teenagers should be given Scripture verses to meditate upon and memorize on a weekly basis. The truth of these verses will sustain them in the hour of temptation.

APPLY GOD'S WORD
"Take heed unto thyself…"
I Timothy 4:16

A Bible-based youth ministry will help young people to apply God's Word in their daily lives. So many times we emphasize the *why* without ever mentioning the *how*. Teenagers need to be taught *how* to pray, *how* to study the Bible, *how* to win souls, *how* to fight sin, and *how* to serve the Lord with their lives.

It was once said, "Other books were given for information, but the Bible was given for our transformation." This transformation will only begin when we make application of the Scriptures. Teenagers should not only be instructed to listen to the Word of God, but also to live it out. Joshua 1:8, ***"This book of the law shall not depart out of thy mouth; but thou shalt meditate therein day and night, that thou mayest observe to do according to all that is written therein: for then thou shalt make thy way prosperous, and then thou shalt have good success."***

When we put the Bible back into the teen ministry, young people will find purpose, direction, and vision for life. The youth leader, with an open Bible, can say to any teenager, *"...This is the way, walk ye in it..."* (Isaiah 30:21).

Giving the Word of God its proper place will produce a healthy youth ministry for the glory of God. We need not complain about the Ten Commandments being taken out of the public school until we are willing to put the Bible back into our youth ministries!

CHAPTER 2

BIBLICAL PREACHING AND TEACHING TO TEENAGERS

Contrary to what we may believe, teenagers respond to the strong preaching and straightforward teaching of the Bible. The plain truth, when bathed in love and prayer, is openly accepted among the majority of teenagers. Most young people appreciate anyone who will tell them the truth.

God has chosen the methods of preaching and teaching to communicate biblical truth to mankind. I Corinthians 1:21 says, ***"...It pleased God by the foolishness of preaching to save them that believe."*** II Timothy 2:2 says, ***"...The same commit thou to faithful men, who shall be able to teach others also."*** Both teaching and preaching will accomplish several goals.

- Teaching will *burden* you; preaching will *bother* you.
- Teaching will *capture the mind;* preaching will *change the heart.*
- Teaching leaves you *concerned*; preaching leaves you *corrected.*
- Teaching *furnishes facts*; preaching *forces a decision.*
- Teaching *satisfies a need;* preaching *strikes a nerve.*

There are several practical pointers to consider when teaching or preaching to teenagers.

BE BIBLICAL IN YOUR MESSAGE

II Timothy 3:16 says, *"All scripture is given by inspiration of God, and is profitable for doctrine, for reproof, for correction, for instruction in righteousness."*

In a lifetime of youth ministry, we can never exhaust the depths of the Bible. The Bible itself is a divine library of sixty-six volumes containing law, history, poetry, prophecy, wisdom, literature, narratives, allegories, parables, biographies, dramas, riddles, visions, sermons, songs, conversations, letters, and teachings. The 1,189 chapters, the 31,176 verses, and the 2,930 Bible characters provide adequate resource material from which to speak to teenagers for a lifetime.

> Declaring the eternal truths of God's Word will not always be popular, but it will certainly be profitable.

Communicating the Word of God to young people in an accurate and compelling manner is the high calling of the youth minister. Teenagers need practical answers to life's daily problems and pressures. The Bible provides these answers. Declaring the eternal truths of God's Word will not always be *popular*, but it will certainly be *profitable*.

HAVE A FIRM KNOWLEDGE OF YOUR SUBJECT

"That which we have seen and heard declare we unto you..." (I John 1:3). Be careful about *public speech* without *private study*. It is good to be well prepared when addressing teenagers with biblical truth. Allow the main truth of your subject to grip your own heart in such a way that every listener is moved toward God. The preacher and teacher of the Bible must *exemplify* in his life what he *expounds* with his lips.

> The preacher and teacher of the Bible must *exemplify* in his life what he *expounds* with his lips.

BE EXCITED ABOUT YOUR SUBJECT

Enthusiasm is contagious! As you communicate the Word of God, realize that you are a thermostat rather than a thermometer. You must take a part in setting the temperature and not just merely recording it. Teenagers want to hear someone who is excited about what they are saying. It was John Wesley who said, "I just set myself on fire and folks come to watch me as I burn." Abraham Lincoln said, "When I hear a man preaching, I like to see him act as if he were fighting bees."[2] Do not have the reputation of being a boring speaker. Ask the Lord for a double dose of joy and excitement!

MAKE GOOD USE OF ILLUSTRATIONS

When speaking to teenagers, we should seek to do three things with each point of a sermon or lesson: make the point, illustrate it, and apply it. One of the most neglected or misused elements of teaching is illustration.

Illustration is a way to visualize the truth we seek to present. A good illustration will shed light on the subject at hand. A sermon without illustration is like a house without windows.

MAKE APPLICATION OF EVERY POINT

James 1:22 says, ***"But be ye doers of the word, and not hearers only, deceiving your own selves."*** Teach young people how to apply biblical truth to their individual lives. C. H. Spurgeon said that the sermon does not begin until the application begins. This application should always be personal to the listener. Teenagers should be exhorted to put into practice what they have learned.

C.H. Spurgeon said that the sermon does not begin until the application begins.

CHAPTER 3

BIBLICAL COUNSELING OF TEENAGERS

Psalm 1:1 says, ***"Blessed is the man that walketh not in the counsel of the ungodly, nor standeth in the way of sinners, nor sitteth in the seat of the scornful."*** Webster defines the word *counsel* in this way: "to advise; to steer or guide with advice."[3] Counseling has also been considered "an exchanging of ideas or values." Counseling focuses on individual needs. It allows for two-way communication.

Proper counseling is very important when dealing with young people, for it is in the teenage years that some of life's most important decisions are made. When counseling young people, we must remember that we are God's representatives. We have within our grasp the opportunity to influence lives for time and eternity. Teens need more than just a listening ear. They need Bible answers for life's problems.

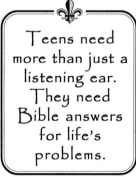

Teens need more than just a listening ear. They need Bible answers for life's problems.

There are times when you will feel utterly convinced that you do not have what it takes to counsel young people. No matter how uninformed, ill-equipped, or unqualified we may feel, we are still confronted with the questions and problems that our teens are facing today. Though every counseling session is different, there are some practical things we can consider in every situation.

BE FAMILIAR WITH COMMON PROBLEMS

The most common teenage problems will usually fall into one of four categories:

1. *Spiritual problems* - Assurance of salvation, backsliding, habitual sin, temptations, immorality, decisions...
2. *Social problems* - Friendships, self-esteem, peer pressure, runaway attempts, anger, jealousy...
3. *Relational problems* - Love, dating, choosing for marriage, parental divorce, single parent family, loneliness, contending with peer rejection...
4. *Vocational problems* - Knowing God's will, choosing a career or ministry, choosing a college...

BE PREPARED FOR MORE SERIOUS PROBLEMS

More serious problems would include pre-marital sex, suicidal tendencies, drug experimentation, pornography/perversion, gang involvement, drinking/smoking, running away, crime, etc. Research tells a statistical horror story of what is happening every day in America[4]:

- 2,900 teens get pregnant
- 1,106 teenage girls have an abortion
- 4,219 teens contract a sexually transmitted disease
- 6 teenagers commit suicide
- 3,288 teenagers run away from home
- 2,989 children see their parents divorced
- 1,512 teenagers drop out of school
- 7,742 teenagers become sexually active
- 372 teenage girls have a miscarriage

ASK GOD FOR WISDOM

James 1:5 says, *"If any of you lack wisdom, let him ask of God, that giveth to all men liberally, and upbraideth not; and it shall be given him."* *Wisdom* is "the ability and willingness to base all of our thoughts, actions, and decisions, on the principles of the Word of God."[5] Asking God for wisdom should be a common practice before any counseling session.

MAKE YOURSELF AVAILABLE

Teenagers need to feel that the youth leader is approachable and available at all times. We should never be so busy that we neglect the needs and concerns of our young people. Learn how to give counsel in a casual setting. Some of the best times for counseling are after church in the parking lot, in the church pew, in the bus while driving, in the car while soul winning, or even on a youth activity. You do not have to be behind a desk in the office to be successful in counseling.

INFORM THE PARENTS BEFORE COUNSELING

Find out where the parent stands before giving advice to the teenager. Be careful not to contradict the advice of a Christian parent. This is a line we should never cross. In doing so, we could be accused of causing division in the home. We must be sensitive to the parents' Biblical and legal authority over the young person. Any effort to advise or guide a teen without the knowledge, approval, or involvement of the parent is unwise.

HAVE SCHEDULED APPOINTMENTS

Try to schedule these appointments during the week at the church office. When scheduling the appointment, ask the young person about the topic you will be discussing. This will give you time to pray and, if necessary, research.

SET THEM AT EASE

It is good to begin the session with prayer. This will establish the presence of Christ. Learn also to use small talk. This will break the ice and set the tone for open communication.

LISTEN ATTENTIVELY WITHOUT INTERRUPTION

By giving your individual attention while they are sharing their problem, you are saying that they are important to you and that you earnestly share their burden. Listening to all of their problems will help you to avoid making hasty conclusions.

NEVER APPEAR SHOCKED BY WHAT THEY SAY

Sometimes teenagers will share with you the tip of the iceberg to see your reaction. If you overreact, they may never feel comfortable about discussing sin problems of a serious nature. Teenagers need to know that their world has not come to an end because of one difficult mistake. Expressing shock may temporarily block your counseling progress.

DO NOT ACCEPT EVERYTHING YOU HEAR AS TOTAL TRUTH

There is very often another side to every story. Many counselors fail by coming to conclusions too quickly. Proverbs 18:13 says, *"He that answereth a matter before he heareth it, it is folly and shame unto him."*

DO NOT ASK FOR DETAILS OF IMMORALITY

The Bible says to be *"simple concerning evil"* (Romans 16:19). Some things can be understood without being spoken.

BE CAREFUL WHEN WITH THE OPPOSITE SEX

Take as many precautions as possible. Some safeguarding tips to follow are:
- Have your wife/husband present when possible.
- Have a window or door ajar if possible.
- Never touch anyone to offer comfort.
- Have a box of tissues available.
- Have your desk separating you and the counselee.

ASK QUESTIONS TO FIND THE ROOT OF THE PROBLEM

A good question to begin with would be: "How do you feel about what you have done?" Right questions will reveal the conscience of the teenager. Most problems can be traced back to the neglect of one or more of the following areas of the Christian life:
- Reading the Bible
- Prayer
- Faithful church attendance
- Tithing/giving
- Witnessing
- Christian service

USE THE BIBLE WHEN ADDRESSING PROBLEMS

Real counseling involves the imparting of information. The Holy Spirit uses the counselor to correct human problems by the application of God's Word. Because the counselor is capable of solving his own problems spiritually, he is qualified to help others do so. When counseling teens, do not use terms like "I think" or "I feel." This allows the teen to leave and say it was just your opinion. Use statements that establish authority; for example, "God has shown me from His Word." God's Word should be the authority in the counseling session.

> God's Word should be the authority in the counseling session.

WRITE OUT A PRESCRIPTION FOR THEM TO FOLLOW

Do not just diagnose the problem, offer them a cure for their ailment. For example:
- Read Romans 6
- Pray 5 minutes a day
- No TV for one week
- Attend every service this month

SCHEDULE ANOTHER APPOINTMENT IF NECESSARY

If you are in over your head in a counseling session, ask them if you can pray about it and discuss it at the next appointment. Seek the Lord and pastoral leadership for wisdom.

REPORT CRIMINAL ACTS

If during the counseling session you discover that a criminal act has been committed against the teenager or by the teenager, you have a legal obligation to report it to the pastor and the proper authorities.

ALWAYS REVIEW WHAT YOU SAID BEFORE THEY LEAVE

It is so important to remind those you are counseling not only of what was said but the meaning behind what was said. Remember these three rules:

1. People do not hear what you *say;* they hear what they want to hear.
2. People do not remember what you said; they remember what they *think* you said.
3. People do not repeat what you said; they repeat what they think you *meant.*

NEVER CHANGE YOUR ATTITUDE TOWARD THEM IN PUBLIC

People should not be able to notice a change in your attitude toward them after a counseling session has taken place. Help them get past any awkwardness they may feel.

FOLLOW UP WITH A FRIENDLY LETTER OF REASSURANCE

Write a personal letter to let them know that you are praying for them. Remind them that God is able to forgive our failures and restore us to a place of fellowship once again.

SURVEYING THE LAND

An important step in any work of construction is to take a survey of the land. A wise builder will view the overall picture, checking for the low spots, the high spots, and the obstacles. He is not *discouraged* over that which is crooked; he knows it can be straightened. He is not *detoured* by the obstacles; he exercises patience in removing them. He is not *disappointed* over what is too low; he knows it can be brought up to standard. The Bible says in Isaiah 40:3-4, *"...Prepare ye the way of the LORD, make straight in the desert a highway for our God. Every valley shall be exalted, and every mountain and hill shall be made low: and the crooked shall be made straight, and the rough places plain."*

A successful youth leader must see the overall picture in working with teens. He must acquire a general knowledge of those he has chosen to work with. As he surveys the land, he not only must be burdened over the condition of the fields, but must be optimistic about the job that lies ahead. The wise youth leader will understand his mission, taking joy in the opportunity afforded him to influence lives for eternity.

CHAPTER 4

THE VITAL NECESSITY OF THE LOCAL CHURCH YOUTH MINISTRY

Ecclesiastes 11:9-12:1, *"Rejoice, O young man, in thy youth; and let thy heart cheer thee in the days of thy youth, and walk in the ways of thine heart, and in the sight of thine eyes: but know thou, that for all these things God will bring thee into judgment. Therefore remove sorrow from thy heart, and put away evil from thy flesh: for childhood and youth are vanity. Remember now thy Creator in the days of thy youth, while the evil days come not, nor the years draw nigh, when thou shalt say, I have no pleasure in them."*

The most important days of life are lived in the days of our youth. At the turn of the 21st century, there were over 22 million teenagers living in America between the ages of 13 and 19.[6] This generation of young people are, in many respects, more fortunate than any other generation that has ever lived. They are better educated, better fed, better housed, better clothed, and more sophisticated than any of their predecessors.

> Satan has targeted the lives of young people like never before.

However, this generation of young people is also faced with more temptations, more difficulties, and more problems than can ever be imagined. Our teenagers are up against a host of sins and pitfalls that many adults have never faced. Satan has targeted the lives of young people like never before. I Peter 5:8 says, ***"Be sober, be vigilant; because your adversary the devil, as a roaring lion, walketh about, seeking whom he may devour."*** The word *devour* means *"to make disappear."* The devil has been very successful in these last days at removing young people from God's plan and purpose for their lives.

THE CRISIS OF AMERICA'S YOUTH

There are four problems facing the young people of America:

1. Misinformed Minds

The attack of the devil is upon the mind of the teenager. Teens are being taught that there is no right or wrong and that there are no absolutes in life. This mindset is a direct result of the secular humanism and pluralism that is pushed in our society. It has found its way into the public school system and has crept unaware into the realm of religion. The minds of young people are being slowly corrupted by the teachings of evolution and reincarnation. The influence of rock music, pornography, and the liberal media have all played a part in polluting the minds of American youth.

- 68% of American youth have unsupervised access to the internet.
- 17.5 million teen internet surfers have visited pornography websites at least once.
- The average American teen owns at least 40 musical CD's.
- The average American teen watches TV about 3 hours each day.
- Between grades 7 and 12, the average teen listens to 10,500 hours of rock music.[7]

During a recent survey of the lyrics of the top 20 best-selling rock, hip-hop, and rap disks; it was discovered that:

- 100% of the feature songs celebrated illicit sex and drug abuse.
- 89% of the songs portrayed suicide as a visible option.
- 77% of the songs mocked authority figures.
- 61% of the songs profiled violent acts such as rape, murder, and molestation.

- 28% of the songs criticized religion and Christianity.[8]

The Bible used to be the standard of truth in America. Now, every man does what is right in his own eyes.

2. Misused Bodies

Many young people have yielded their bodies as instruments of unrighteousness unto sin (Romans 6:13).
- 38% of American highschoolers are chain smokers
- 51% of American highschoolers drink alcohol
- 48% of American highschoolers have become sexually immoral
- 1,392 kids will attempt suicide every day in America
- 672 teen girls will give birth out of wedlock every day in America
- 1,056 teen girls will have abortions every day in America[9]

3. Misplaced Confidence

The average American teenager has made heroes out of those people who mock the God of the Holy Bible. They have made idols out of idiots. Psalm 118:8 says, ***"It is better to trust in the LORD than to put confidence*** *in man.*" Young people have given their affection, admiration, and confidence to the poorest of all role models. One recent survey asked teenagers to name a list of their heroes. At the top of the list were sports figures, singers, and hollywood entertainers. There were no artists, architects, authors, doctors, politicians, preachers, teachers, or missionaries.

4. Misspent Energies

The fourth problem America's youth has is *misspent energies*. Many young people are spending their lives in pursuit of unworthy goals. The best years of their life are spent chasing after the pleasures of this world. The emphasis today is not upon what is right but upon what feels good. Like the prodigal of the Bible, many are seeking fulfillment from the far country instead of from the Father's house.

Never in human history has there been a greater need for a life-changing ministry to teenagers than today. Teenagers have *failures* to overcome, *fears* to be addressed, *families* to be reached, a *faith* to be challenged, and a *future* to be inspired. God has designed the local church to address the needs of young people in this generation.

THE COMMITMENT OF THE LOCAL CHURCH YOUTH MINISTRY

To make a difference in the lives of young people, the youth ministry must undertake the four-fold commitment found in Ezekiel 34:16, *"I will seek that which was lost, and bring again that which was driven away, and will bind up that which was broken, and will strengthen that which was sick: but I will destroy the fat and the strong; I will feed them with judgment."*

1. The youth ministry must seek that which is lost.

We need no new commission from our Lord. We are commanded by Christ Jesus to seek after the souls of men. John 20:21, *"Then said Jesus to them again, Peace be unto you: as my Father hath sent me, even so send I you."* This duty is necessary not only because it is the command of the Lord, but also because of the condition of the lost.

- Lost young people are perishing. John 3:16, *"For God so loved the world, that he gave his only begotten Son, that* whosoever believeth in him should not perish, but have everlasting life."

- Lost young people are under God's wrath. John 3:36, *"He that believeth on the Son hath everlasting life: and he that believeth not the Son shall not see life; but the wrath of God abideth on him."*

- Lost young people are without hope. Ephesians 2:12, *"That at that time ye were without Christ, being aliens from the commonwealth of Israel, and strangers from the covenants of promise, having no hope, and without God in the world."*

- Lost young people are blinded by the devil. II Corinthians 4:3-4, *"But if our gospel be hid, it is hid to them that are lost: In whom the god of this world hath blinded the minds of them which believe not, lest the light of the glorious gospel of Christ, who is the image of God, should shine unto them."*

- Lost young people are dead in sin. Ephesians 2:1, *"And you hath he quickened, who were dead in trespasses and sins."*

- Lost young people are on the road to hell. Matthew 7:13, *"Enter ye in at the strait gate: for wide is the gate, and broad is the way, that leadeth to destruction, and many there be which go in thereat:"*

2. The youth ministry must bring again that which is driven away.

The Word of God says in Matthew 18:10-14, *"Take heed that ye despise not one of these little ones; for I say unto you, That in heaven their angels do always behold the face of my Father which is in heaven. For the Son of man is come to save that which was lost. How think ye? If a man have an hundred sheep, and one of them be gone astray, doth he not leave the ninety and nine, and goeth into the mountains, and seeketh that which is gone astray? And if so be that he find it, verily I say unto you, he rejoiceth more of that sheep, than of the ninety and nine which went not astray. Even so it is not the will of your Father which is in heaven, that one of these little ones should perish."*

If we are to have the spirit of the Good Shepherd, we must seek those who have gone astray. What are the reasons that teenagers are driven away from church?

- Some become offended. Matthew 18:6, *"But whoso shall offend one of these little ones which believe in me, it were better for him that a millstone were hanged about his neck, and that he were drowned in the depth of the sea."*
- Some get in the wrong crowd. Luke 15:15, *"And he went and joined himself to a citizen of that country; and he sent him into his fields to feed swine."*
- Some have no encouragement from home. Colossians 3:21, *"Fathers, provoke not your children to anger, lest they be discouraged."*
- Some are victims of circumstances. Psalm 27:13, *"I had fainted, unless I had believed to see the goodness of the LORD in the land of the living."*

3. The youth ministry must bind up that which is broken.

When we speak to the broken-hearted, we will never lack an audience.

> When we speak to the broken-hearted, we will never lack an audience.

Our youth ministries are filled with broken hearts and lives. The local church youth ministry should always be sensitive and compassionate to those who have "messed up" their lives. Failure is not final with God. Teenagers are longing for a place where they can find forgiveness and healing. This was the ministry of our Lord and should be the goal of the local church. Luke 4:18 says, ***The Spirit of the Lord is upon me, because he hath anointed me to preach the gospel to the poor; he hath sent me to heal the brokenhearted, to preach deliverance to the captives, and recovering of sight to the blind, to set at liberty them that are bruised.***"

4. The youth ministry must strengthen those that remain.

III John 4 says, *"I have no greater joy than to hear that my children walk in truth."* Thank God for the young people in our ministries that continually walk in truth. Not every teen has drifted into the far country. Some have remained faithful in the Father's house and deserve the praise and attention of leadership.

CHAPTER 5

UNDERSTANDING TODAY'S TEENAGER

Someone said that trying to understand a teenager is like trying to nail Jell-O to a tree. However true, before we understand what a teenager is, we must see what he is not. A teenager is not a child, nor is he an adult. He is halfway up the stairs and halfway down the stairs. On one hand, the teenage years are a time of great promise and challenge, but on the other hand, they are a time of great trials and pitfalls.

Jesus understood what it was like to be a teenager. Our Lord could have come into this world as an adult, but He chose to be born in a manger. He deemed it necessary to go through all seven teenage years in order to know our sorrow and be acquainted with our grief. He has been there. As a teenager, he knew what it was like to have a stepfather (Joseph). He had brothers and sisters. *"Is not this the carpenter's son? is not his mother called Mary? and his brethren, James, and Joses, and Simon, and Judas? And his sisters, are they not all with us? Whence then hath this man all these things?"* (Matthew 13:55-56). He had a mother that became upset with Him (when He was lost for three days). He was often misunderstood. He was doubted by many. He often offended people with His truthful words. We can advise any teenager who feels disappointed to look unto Jesus. He understands what teenagers are going through in life.

TEN CHARACTERISTICS OF TEENAGERS

1. Teenagers are Ever-changing

"A time to weep, and a time to laugh; a time to mourn, and a time to dance" (Ecclesiastes 3:4). The teenage years are a period of transition, a bridge between the dependance of childhood and the interdependance of adulthood. Their bodies are changing, and their priorities are changing. There are also emotional changes, educational changes, philosophy changes, and spiritual changes. One day he loves; the next day he hates. One day he is quiet and uncommunicative; the next day he has a tongue that jaywalks over every conversation within his range. The Bible describes this ever-changing period even in the life of Christ: *"And Jesus increased in wisdom and stature, and in favour with God and man"* (Luke 2:52).

2. Teenagers are Impressionable

"He that walketh with wise men shall be wise: but a companion of fools shall be destroyed" (Proverbs 13:20). The teenage years are the stage where values and philosophies are molded. Life's habits are formed during the teen years. Any person who makes an effort to influence the life of a teenager, whether he be a good example or a bad example, usually succeeds. This responsibility must fall squarely upon the shoulders of the parent and spiritual leader. *"Train up a child in the way he should go: and when he is old, he will not depart from it"* (Proverbs 22:6).

3. Teenagers are Self-Conscious

"Which of you by taking thought can add one cubit unto his stature?" (Matthew 6:27). Sometimes a terrible inferiority complex affects the teenager. Think of what they have to face: acne, body odor, braces, voice changes, shaving, hairstyles, allowances, dating, driver's license, jobs, etc. These are just a few things that make a teenager self-conscious. Today's teenager is very sensitive concerning these areas. We must teach them to accept their *appearance*, their *abilities*, and the *adversities* that God has given to them in life.

4. Teenagers are Underestimated

"And Saul said to David, Thou art not able to go against this Philistine to fight with him: for thou art but a youth,and he a man of war from his youth" (I Samuel 17:33). When David volunteered to fight Goliath, King Saul underestimated David's courage and ability. When Goliath looked down and saw David, the Bible says that *"...he disdained him: for he was but a youth..."* (I Samuel 17:42). Here are two men, King Saul and Goliath, who, if given another chance, would never underestimate a teenager again. D.L. Moody often said, "The world has yet to see what God could do with one person who is totally dedicated to him." Do not ever underestimate the potential of a teenager!

> There is a remnant of young people all over America just waiting to be challenged to do something great for God with their lives.

5. Teenagers are Excitable and Enthusiastic

"Rejoice, O young man, in thy youth; and let thy heart cheer thee in the days of thy youth..." (Ecclesiastes 11:9). Young people love excitement. Some are even excited about serving God! Much of this energy and enthusiasm can be channeled into an

area of Christian service. There is a remnant of young people all over America just waiting to be challenged to do something great for God with their lives.

6. Teenagers are Rebellious

"...This hath been thy manner from thy youth, that thou obeyedst not my voice." (Jeremiah 22:21). Rebellion comes from our sinful nature. Every teen has some form of rebellion whether it is open or hidden. The Bible says having this defiant spirit is *"as the sin of witchcraft"* (I Samuel 15:23). The story of the prodigal son teaches us that rebellion affects every relationship in life. It affects the teenager himself. It

> The devil aims every weapon in hell at the teenager in an attempt to ruin their life forever.

affects his family and friends. Most importantly, rebellion affects his relationship with God. Dealing with rebellion, in any form, is a top priority in helping teenagers.

7. Teenagers Face Many Temptations

"Flee also youthful lusts: but follow righteousness, faith, charity, peace, with them that call on the Lord out of a pure heart" (II Timothy

2:22). The devil aims every weapon in hell at the teenager in an attempt to ruin their life forever. Rock music, drugs, sex, pornography, smoking, drinking, dancing, gangs, etc., are just a few of the sins that tempt the teenager. Their only hope is in God. I Corinthians 10:13 says, ***"There hath no temptation taken you but such as is common to man: but God is faithful, who will not suffer you to be tempted above that ye are able; but will with the temptation also make a way to escape, that ye may be able to bear it."***

8. Teenagers are Daring and Like to Try New Things

The local church youth ministry must seek to harness this pioneering spirit of teenagers and challenge them to boldly attempt the extraordinary for God.

"And such as do wickedly against the covenant shall he corrupt by flatteries: but the people that do know their God shall be strong, and do exploits" (Daniel 11:32). In their attempt to be independent, teens will try anything new. They will throw caution to the wind. Whether it is bungee jumping, roller coasting, cliff climbing, or snow skiing, the teenager is a true pioneer. He lives for the moment.

The local church youth ministry must seek to *harness* this pioneering spirit of teenagers and challenge them to boldly attempt the extraordinary for God. Young people who are filled with the Spirit of God are often more courageous in their faith and testimony than most adults in our churches.

9. Teenagers Need Acceptance

"To the praise of the glory of his grace, wherein he hath made us accepted in the beloved" (Ephesians 1:6). In order to fit in, they will sacrifice their hairstyle, their clothing, their music, their heroes, and anything else upon the altar of acceptability. Many are being *"conformed to this world"* instead of being *"transformed"* to the image of Christ.

The key to understanding and ministering to teens is to accept them where they are. There is a "right crowd" in every youth department that should work hard at reaching out to new teenagers. To know that they can be accepted will bring about opportunity for change.

Teens need to know that they are *loved*. This love must be demonstrated through the heart and ministries of the local church. Teens need someone "just to be there for them" in times of sorrow, lonliness, and achievement. Our Savior said, *"...I will never leave thee, nor forsake thee."* (Hebrews 13:5)

10. Teenagers Need Guidance

"There is a way which seemeth right unto a man, but the end thereof are the ways of death" (Proverbs 14:12). Finding the will of God is difficult for most teenagers. The youth leader, with Bible in hand, must help the young person in choosing the right path of life. We must help them *desire* God's will, *discover* God's will, and *do* God's will with their life! Even David recognized a need for guidance when he said, *"Teach me thy way, O LORD, and lead me in a plain path..."* (Psalm 27:11). Later he testifies, *"...He will be our guide even unto death"* (Psalm 48:14). Many young people end up at the wrong destination in life because they listened to the wrong advice along the way.

When we seek to guide the teenager in the will of God, we are faced with much competition. Many times an ungodly friend, a humanistic guidance counselor, an atheistic teacher, lost parents, and even carnal Christians are used of the devil to steer the teenager off course. The youth leader must be assured in his own heart that the Lord has a plan and purpose for every life. God has called us to challenge young people to give their lives to do His will. George W. Truett made a memorable statement about the will of God. He said, "To know the will of God is the greatest knowledge; to do the will of God is the greatest achievement."

> God has called us to challenge young people to give their lives to do His will.

CHAPTER 6

REACHING THE PUBLIC SCHOOL TEENAGER FOR CHRIST

Very little effort is given to reaching the public school teenager for Christ, especially from the local church with a Christian school. A well-constructed youth program will attempt to reach every teen where he is.

Of the 22 million young people in America between the ages of thirteen to nineteen, only a small percentage are enrolled in a Christian/private school. The majority of teens are found in the public school system. In our city of Cape Coral, there are 65,000 young people enrolled in our public schools (2004-2005).[10] Many are walking *"in the counsel of the ungodly,"* standing *"in the way of sinners,"* and sitting *"in the seat of the scornful"* (Psalm 1:1).

The public schools of America are the mission fields that are so often neglected.

The public schools of America are the mission fields that are so often neglected. If we are going to impact America for God, we must aggressively pursue the public school teenager with the gospel of Christ.

IMPACTING THE PUBLIC SCHOOL TEENAGER

1. Develop an Evangelistic Sunday School Class

The evangelistic Sunday school not only teaches the Bible, but it also reaches the lost. *Reaching* and *teaching* are the two tracks upon which the Sunday school train must be run. Practice open enrollment. This means anyone, anytime, anywhere can be enrolled in the teen Sunday school class. Teenagers do not have to be a member of the church in order to be a member of the teen class. After their name is on the roll, go after them, get them saved, baptize them, and teach them all things in the Bible. We must remember the old philosophy of "reaching the reachable and teaching the teachable." This is God's plan, and it still works. ***"Go ye therefore, and teach all nations, baptizing them in the name of the Father, and of the Son, and of the Holy Ghost: Teaching them to observe all things whatsoever I have commanded you: and, lo, I am with you alway, even unto the end of the world. Amen"*** (Matthew 28:19-20).

2. Provide an Atmosphere where Public School Teens feel Welcome

We are not to change the ministry to fit the world. Yet, the youth leader should create an atmosphere where lost teenagers feel welcomed enough to hear and receive the gospel of Christ. We must realize that our *disposition* turns more young people away than our *position*. Public school teenagers should not feel like third-class members. Learn to speak to them at every service. Provide a Bible for those who come to church without one. Give them a copy of a monthly youth calendar. Play an occasional game in Sunday school. Encourage them to bring their friends to church and make a big deal of it when they come!

> We must realize that our *disposition* turns more young people away than our *position*.

3. Accept People where They are

Public school teens have problems. Boys may come with earrings and necklaces, while girls may come with purple hair and immodest clothing. We must never forget that every soul can be won to Christ. Only the Lord can transform lives. We must accept

people where they are and then point them to what
God wants them to become. I would rather have a
Sunday school class with public school teenagers
desiring to be like Jesus, than to have a room full of
Christian school teens desiring to be like the world.
Our Lord was criticized for loving the lost, and we
must also expect a measure of criticism. *"And the
Pharisees and scribes murmured, saying, This man
receiveth sinners, and eateth with them"* (Luke
15:2). Do not let the Pharisee in the pew hinder you
from reaching the lost. Accept teenagers where they
are. This means to treat them with kindness, showing
a genuine love for their soul. Set them at ease and
never embarrass them. When a teenager feels loved,
walls will come down and progress for ministry can
begin.

4. Use Sunday School Campaigns and Special Days

Teens love competition. Challenge them to bring
visitors from their public school to church. Have a
contest between the different schools during each
campaign with prizes for each teen bringing the most
visitors. One year our "Sunday School Super Bowl"
campaign produced forty visitors during a six-week
period. Use special days to the fullest.

5. Start Bible Clubs in the Public Schools

The Supreme Court has approved the *"Equal Access Act"* for any Christian teen that desires to have a Bible club in their school. This act forbids discrimination by schools against any students who wish to conduct a meeting within the limited open forum on the basis of the religious, political, philosophical, or other content of the speech.[11] To start a Bible club:

- Find several teens, preferably in your church, who are interested in starting a Bible study in the junior or senior high school they attend.
- Meet with the principal or an adult teacher who is willing to be a sponsor.
- Acquire a meeting place for your club either before, during, or after school. (Take what you can get at the start.)
- Have a name for your club and give a stated purpose for your existence. (One example is the A.C.T.S. Club, which stands for Active Christians in Today's Schools.)
- Use these clubs to promote Bible study, prayer, devotions, fellowship, singing, activities, and of course, evangelism.

The Temple Baptist Church in Powell, TN has been very successful in starting Bible clubs in the junior high and senior high schools of Knox County. Contact them about the *"Teens for Christ"* Bible club program.[12]

6. Visit Teens at the Public School Bus Stops

As early as six o'clock in the morning, there are hundreds of teens waiting to catch the bus to school. Increase their burden for reaching the lost and enlist homeschoolers in your church to help you visit these public school bus stops. Design an attractive teen tract or flyer that can be passed out to every teen. An effective way to get their name and address is to have a section that they fill out, tear off, and mail back to the church. Purchase a "postage paid" stamp to assure a higher response.

> To reach the public school teen, we must show a genuine interest in their lives.

7. Attend Public School Functions and Sporting Events

To reach the public school teen, we must show a genuine interest in their lives. This may involve eating a meal in the lunchroom, participating in the *National Day of Prayer* (See You at the Pole), or even attending an occasional football, basketball, or baseball game. Use this time to meet parents, friends, teachers, principals, and coaches and build relationships with them. Always have a business card or tract to give to the adults you meet. A situation will one day arise where they will need someone to call for advice or help for the teenager.

8. Plan an Occasional Youth Activity that Appeals to the Public School Teenager

We should never fall into the trap of only providing activities for the dedicated, sold-out, Christian teenagers of our church. If a year passes on your youth calendar and you have not had one lost young person attend a youth activity, then you have missed the boat. You no longer have a youth "ministry", you now have a youth "group."

Plan an activity , on the church property if possible, that centers on evangelism and not just fellowship. An evangelistic film, a Friday night youth rally, an overnight lock-in (with plenty of supervision) are just a few ideas that work in introducing the public school teen to your youth ministry. Always give the gospel at these activities. Cast the net and trust God for the increase. After an evangelistic activity, you will have months of follow-up work to accomplish from the visitors who attended.

9. Be Relevant in your Teaching and Preaching

There is always the great challenge of keeping the interest of young people. Topics such as suicide, abortion, rock music, evolution, dating, and the will of God should be discussed throughout the year. We do not have to compromise the truth to reach the public school teenager. If you speak the truth in love, teens will love and respect you for it. Teenagers are searching for the truth. God's Word has the answers. In Psalm 107:20 the Bible says, ***"He sent his word, and healed them, and delivered them from their destructions."*** If they do not hear the truth in church, where will they hear it?

10. Acquire a Public School Enrollment List

This computer list of students is hard to come by, but it does exist. The military uses it to recruit graduates into the service. I acquired a list of everyone in the eleventh grade at one of our high schools. There were 380 names and addresses on this list. I sent them a letter and information about the youth group along with a personal invitation to attend. The response was great.

> We do not have to compromise the truth to reach the public school teenager.

11. Start a Teen Van Route on Sundays

The teenager who just got saved is a great prospect to help build a teen route. Take them to visit on Saturdays and fill up the van with their friends from school.

12. Designate a "Teen Section" in the Sunday Morning Worship Service

Young people enjoy being together in church. If you do not designate an area for them to sit, they will usually end up on the back row. It is best for the teens to have a section in the front of the church on Sunday morning. This gives the pastor an opportunity to address the youth group as a whole, and it also makes every teen visitor feel welcome. During the invitation, the teenager is just a few steps away from the altar.

13. Involve Church Members in the Youth Ministry who Work in the Public School System

In most counties, the public school is the number one employer. There are teachers, coaches, bus drivers, etc. in our churches who have a deep burden for young people because they see them on a regular basis. They are eye-witnesses of the struggles and pitfalls that public school teenagers are facing. They are standing in the frontlines. These adults can be recruited, trained, and challenged to make a real difference in the lives of teens by serving in the local church youth ministry.

We must never forget that the public school is not our enemy; it is our mission field!

SECTION III

SUPERVISING THE PROJECT

The supervisor of the construction project is ultimately responsible for its overall success or failure. His watchful eye is upon every stage of construction until the very end. As a supervisor, he corrects, motivates, instructs, and encourages those under his leadership. He takes painstaking care in the details and deadlines of the work of construction. He is willing to work through any problem that arises, knowing that his compensation is just around the corner. The supervisor sees the overall picture and has a goal towards which he is pressing. He relies upon a faithful crew of workers to aid him in his worthy mission.

In a biblical sense, the local church pastor is the overseer of any ministry in the church. Like the general contractor, he takes the over-sight. In many churches, the supervision of the youth ministry is delegated to a youth director. In such a case, he is given the responsibility to share in the pastor's ministry. As a youth director, he encourages, motivates, instructs, exhorts and reproves those under his care. He is not only a responsible person, but is also someone with whom others enjoy to labor. The youth director surrounds himself with a committed crew of believers that will help him accomplish the work God has given him to do. As the spiritual leader, his watchful eye is upon every facet of the youth ministry, knowing that he must give an account to his pastor, and ultimately, to God at the Judgment Seat of Christ. Though his commitment is sometimes overlooked in this life, his reward is awaiting in the life to come.

CHAPTER 7

THE RESPONSIBILITIES OF THE YOUTH DIRECTOR

Today's youth minister is expected to be all things to all people. Churches usually want someone with the grace of a swan, the gentleness of a dove, the strength of an eagle, the friendliness of a sparrow, the eye of a hawk, the night hours of an owl, while living on the food of a canary. A rare bird like this is hard to find!

Robert Laurent gives an interesting depiction of the position that many youth ministers find themselves in:

- If his hair has any gray in it, he is too old to relate to teenagers. If he is a recent graduate, he hasn't had enough experience for the job.
- If he has any children, he has too many distractions. If he has no children, he can't relate to parents and teens.
- If his wife takes an active role in his ministry, she is a presuming woman and does not know her place. If she does not, she is not interested in the church.

- If he makes close friends, he is cliquish. If he is friendly with everyone, he is insincere and shallow.
- If he considers someday pastoring his own church, he is not committed to helping youth. If he commits himself to youth work for life, it is because he does not have what it takes to be a senior pastor.[13]

EIGHT QUALITIES OF A SUCCESSFUL YOUTH MINISTER

1. He Seizes Every Opportunity to Win Souls

Proverbs 11:30 says, *"The fruit of the righteous is a tree of life; and he that winneth souls is wise."* The successful youth leader must have a burning desire to reach as many people with the gospel as possible. The youth leader must stay on the gospel trail. He witnesses, passes out tracts, supports missionaries, disciples new converts, and preaches and teaches the Word of God. He must also develop and train others in the matter of personal soul winning. At the top of the youth minister's list is the matter of making Christ known to every teenager he possibly can.

2. He Sets Goals in the Youth Ministry

Proverbs 29:18 says, *"Where there is no vision, the people perish: but he that keepeth the law, happy is he."* The youth ministry is not a place for idleness or laziness. A youth minister with vision from God will always have more work to do than he can get done. The youth minister must learn to set yearly, monthly, weekly and daily goals. These visions are planned for attendance and spiritual progress. These goals are to be shared with the pastor, parent, and teenager. His direction is always moving forward in the ministry. The successful youth leader plans ahead. Remember that Noah did not build the ark in the rain!

> The youth ministry is not a place for idleness or laziness.

3. He Serves Others Unconditionally

I Corinthians 9:19 says, *"For though I be free from all men, yet have I made myself servant unto all, that I might gain the more."* Biblical leadership obeys God and serves others. Even though the youth leader is occasionally taken advantage of, he has a servant's heart and love for people that is evident for all to see. The question is not how many people can I lead, but rather how many people can I serve.

4. He Strengthens the Home of the Teenager

Malachi 4:6 says, *"And he shall turn the heart of the fathers to the children, and the heart of the children to their fathers, lest I come and smite the earth with a curse."* The best term to describe the role of a youth minister is the word bridge-builder. He is to direct the teenager first to the Lord Jesus, second to the authority of the parents, and third to the influence of the local church pastor. The successful youth minister does not *compete* with the home; he learns to *complement* the home. He turns the hearts of the teenagers to their parents and the hearts of the parents to the teenagers.

> The successful youth minister does not *compete* with the home; he learns to *complement* the home.

5. He Submits to Pastoral Authority

Hebrews 13:7 says, *"Remember them which have the rule over you, who have spoken unto you the word of God: whose faith follow, considering the end of their conversation."* The youth leader is an extension of the pastor's ministry. He represents the pastor to the teenagers. He should never do or say anything that would bring reproach upon pastoral authority. Successful youth leaders have learned to live surrendered lives to God and to God's authority. A youth minister who refuses to submit to pastoral authority is no different than a rebellious teenager who will not submit to his parent's authority! Brethren, let us practice what we preach and remember that we will reap what we sow.

6. He Stimulates Enthusiasm in Workers and Followers

Colossians 3:23 says, *"And whatsoever ye do, do it heartily, as to the Lord, and not unto men."* Teenagers get excited when their youth leader goes all out for the glory of God. Enthusiasm is contagious! The successful youth leader approaches every activity, project, and event with zeal and excitement. This enthusiasm is not a superficial act; it is the result of the joy of the Lord in his soul.

7. He Seeks the Favour and Blessing of God

Luke 2:52 says, *"And Jesus increased in wisdom and stature, and in favour with God and man."* Just as the Lord Jesus increased in favour with God, the youth leader must desire God's blessing and power upon his life and ministry. Samuel, a successful youth leader in the Bible, *"was in favour both with the LORD, and also with men"* (I Samuel 2:26). This favour makes the difference in a ministry. It turns the average into excellence. It turns the natural into the supernatural.

The favour of God is obtained through *private* prayer (Matthew 6:6), by *practicing* righteousness (Psalm 5:12), by *pursuing* wisdom (Proverbs 8:35), and by *performing* good works (Proverbs 11:27).

8. He is Steadfast in His Commitment to the Youth Ministry

Ecclesiastes 9:10 says, ***"Whatsoever thy hand findeth to do, do it with thy might; for there is no work, nor device, nor knowledge, nor wisdom, in the grave, whither thou goest."*** The successful youth leader does not see the youth ministry as a stepping-stone to greater things. The real measure of success is found in staying somewhere long enough to reap a harvest. Teenagers are looking for someone to stay with them for the long haul. Rarely does a youth minister ever influence a young person from the sixth grade all the way to their high school graduation. It takes time to build anything for the glory of God. Someone who is faithfully plugging away at the basics,

> The real measure of success is found in staying somewhere long enough to reap a harvest.

setting an example of Christian contentment, will reap manifold blessings in the lives of young people.

CHAPTER 8

PAYING THE PRICE FOR SUCCESSFUL YOUTH WORK

I Corinthians 15:58 says, *"Therefore, my beloved brethren, be ye stedfast, unmoveable, always abounding in the work of the Lord, forasmuch as ye know that your labour is not in vain in the Lord."* Dr. Lee Roberson said, "Everything rises and falls on leadership." A real leader will be willing to pay the price when everyone else has given up on the teenager. He is to be a man of responsibility and diligence. Youth leaders must labor and toil even when results are not seen. What is the *"P.R.I.C.E"* we must pay for success?

P-ERSEVERANCE

Proverbs 20:6 says, *"Most men will proclaim every one his own goodness: but a faithful man who can find?"* Webster defines *perseverance* as "steadfastness, to persist in any purpose or enterprise; to continue striving in spite of opposition."[14] Successful youth programs are not built by the fly-by-night youth leader. It takes time to develop a well-balanced, Christ-honoring youth ministry. Teenagers deserve leadership

79

that is willing to pay the price, to go the extra mile, and to stay for the long haul. The average tenure of a youth director in a Baptist church is about 1½ years. After the honeymoon period is over, they feel "led" to begin looking for greener pastures. There are three reasons that cause this to happen:

> The average tenure of a youth director in a Baptist church is about 1.5 years.

1. Problems Gather

Job said, *"Man that is born of a woman is of few days, and full of trouble"* (Job 14:1). Eventually, the "trouble truck" will pull into your driveway. Every worthy effort in the ministry will have its share of problems. The youth leader must be willing to stay and persevere even when the problems seem overwhelming. We must remember that God's promises are always greater than our problems! *"And we know that all things work together for good to them that love God, to them who are the called according to his purpose"* (Romans 8:28).

2. Pressure is Great

The youth ministry is full of daily pressures-teenagers make heartbreaking decisions, parents get upset with the youth director, church members criticize the youth program; not to mention the pressure of fund raising, dealing with problems, and the constant rebuilding and replenishing of the youth ministry. This daily pressure may cause many youth leaders to turn back in the day of battle.

3. Praise is Gone

Jesus warned His disciples of loving the praise of men more than the praise of God. A youth leader who is dead to self will not be affected by criticism or by praise. You can kick him or kiss him, and it does not change his service to the Lord. Soon there is a loss of popularity. The encouraging cards, the pats on the back, the public praise, and the thankful telephone calls will cease to exist. Many youth directors stay just long enough for the icing to be licked off the cake. Teenagers need leaders who are stable and balanced, leaders they can trust to be there for them long-term.

> Many youth directors stay just long enough for the icing to be licked off the cake.

R-ESPONSIBILITY

Hebrews 13:17 says, ***"Obey them that have the rule over you, and submit yourselves: for they watch*** *for your souls, as they that must give account, that they may do it with joy, and not with grief: for that is unprofitable for you.*" A Christian should always be known to be responsible to God and to other people for the work he has to do and for the things that he has to care for. The God-called youth leader must be willing to bear the responsibility of the entire youth ministry. The burden must rest upon his shoulders. Blame-shifting is a common practice in this day and age. The successful youth leader will not shift blame, but will personally take responsibility for the spiritual growth, problems, mistakes, misunderstandings, decisions, and the direction of the youth group God has entrusted to him. The Christian worker will be held responsible at the Judgment Seat of Christ for the work that God has given him to do.

I-nvolvement/Investment

Paying the price to being successful in youth ministry will require personal involvement and investment in the lives of teenagers. It is more than just observing from a distance. It is taking the teenager by the hand and heart and walking him through the difficult problems of the teenage years. It is this individual approach that will make a lasting impact upon a teenager's life. In the long run, this is time well invested. Spiritual investment means we are making personal deposits into someone's life for time and eternity, knowing all the while that our labour *"is not in vain in the Lord"* (I Corinthians 15:58).

C-OMPASSION

Jude 22 says, *"And of some have compassion, making a difference."* Genuine compassion will make the difference in the lives of young people when all else fails. Someone described compassion as "getting their hurt into your heart." A youth worker who is not compassionate has no place in the youth ministry. Compassion is an essential quality to possess when working with people. The Scripture says on many occasions that when Jesus saw the multitudes, He was *"moved with compassion"* on them. A compassionate person is one who has a tender heart toward the needs and sufferings of others and who has a desire to help others.

> Someone described compassion as "getting their hurt into your heart."

E-XCELLENCE

Philippians 1:10 says, *"That ye may approve things that are excellent; that ye may be sincere and without offence till the day of Christ."* Some take the course of least resistance, while others strive for excellence. Paying the price for excellence is not always easy. It involves tough decisions, standards, separation, spiritual maturity, and Scriptural correctness. Striving for excellence should be done in every area of youth ministry. Great youth ministers are those who choose to take the high road in the Christian life. God's way *is* the high way.

We can take the high road of excellence in ministry by:
- *Living* a life that is separated unto the Lord and without reproach (II Corinthians 6:17).
- *Laying* aside weights and sins in our own life to become more effective in ministering to teenagers (Hebrews 12:1-2).
- *Loving* God's will more than our will in life's decisions.
- *Learning* to look beyond what is good and choosing what is best (Philippians 1:9-10).

Perseverance, **R**esponsibility, **I**nvolvement, **C**ompassion, and **E**xcellence - this is the "price" that the successful youth director must be willing to pay.

CHAPTER 9

TRAINING AND DEVELOPING WORKERS

One of the greatest problems in the history of the local church has always been a lack of workers for the ministry. Jesus said unto His disciples in Matthew 9:37-38, *"...The harvest truly is plenteous, but the labourers are few; Pray ye therefore the Lord of the harvest, that he will send forth labourers into his harvest."*

We find four groups of people in the local church: *leaders*, *workers*, *followers*, and *those to be reached*. As we are obedient to the Lord, we will find ourselves moving up the ladder. Those to be reached will become followers, followers will become faithful workers, and eventually workers will become leaders who are responsible for an area of ministry. This is how God's work is to be done in every ministry. We learn this pattern from the Bible. II Timothy 2:2 says, *"And the things that thou hast heard of me among many witnesses, the same commit thou to faithful men, who shall be able to teach others also."* These four groups are given in this verse. Paul is the

> The best way to reach more young people is to involve more workers.

leader; writing to Timothy, the *worker*; who commits to faithful men, *followers*; who are able to teach others also, *those to be reached.*

The best way to reach more young people is to involve more workers. D. L. Moody said, "I'd rather get ten men to do the job, than to do the job of ten men." There are several principles for developing youth workers for the local church ministry. They can be seen in the acrostic *Y.O.U.T.H. W.O.R.K.E.R.S.*

Y-IELD TO THE PASTOR'S ADVICE

In our zealous effort to "get it done," we have all been guilty of *recruiting workers* without *requesting wisdom* from the Lord and the pastor. The pastor is the overseer of every ministry of the local church. It is always best to seek his wisdom *before* selecting a worker. There are two logical reasons for this. First, the pastor knows who would be a great *help*. Second, the pastor knows who would be a great *hinderance*. This approach will save you a lot of trouble down the road. Experience will teach us that it is much

> Experience will teach us that it is much easier to choose the right worker than to get rid of the wrong one.

easier to choose the right worker than to get rid of the wrong one.

O-BSERVE THOSE IN THE CHURCH WHO ARE SETTING THE PROPER EXAMPLE

Always promote what you want to produce. Look for workers who are Christ-honoring examples in conduct and faithfulness. Never allow someone to lead who is unfaithful in their own Christian walk and questionable in their testimony and behavior.

U-SE PEOPLE WHO ENJOY WORKING AND BEING WITH TEENAGERS

The youth ministry is not to be perceived as a burden but as a blessing. Choose workers who have the joy of the Lord and a heart for God. Teens need to know that you can please the Lord and have fun, both at the same time! Our young people will never have a desire for the ministry unless they see someone who enjoys it. On a recent youth activity, we took our young people to the mall for a scavenger hunt with a twist. Instead of the teenagers going through the mall on a search for items to find and bring back, they had to find twelve adult youth

> **Always promote what you want to produce.**

workers from our church who were dressed in disguise while walking through the mall. We disguised ourselves as old men, old women, pregnant women, janitors, police officers, store employees, and tourists. It took the teens nearly two hours to find all of us. The adults had more fun than the teenagers!

T-each and Train Them to be Effective in their Area of Ministry

- Have a weekly or monthly training time for all workers. Be sure to cover the philosophy, purpose, and procedures of the youth ministry in which you are leading. Put these principles in writing and pass them out to every new worker.
- Give them specific responsibilities. You get what you inspect, not what you expect. Be specific. Learn to communicate well to all workers.
- Give the new worker a small assignment in the beginning. Monitor their diligence and character before assigning them any greater responsibility.
- Provide workers with good books and tapes about youth ministry.

- Pray with your workers often. This will allow you to get answers from God, as well as observe the burden of your workers.

H-AVE STANDARDS OF HOLINESS FOR ALL WORKERS AND LEADERS

Leaders and workers should be expected to live holy, separated lives unto the Lord. People who have won personal victories, have lived above reproach, and have come apart from worldliness are the best candidates for workers in the youth ministry. Teenagers need to see an example of Christ-likeness before them. Write out a list of standards that are supported from the Scripture and give it to each youth worker.

> Leaders and workers should be expected to live holy, separated lives unto the Lord.

W-ORK WITH MARRIED COUPLES RATHER THAN SINGLE ADULTS

Teenagers do not need an imitation of themselves. They need a pattern of godly leadership. There is no greater influence that we can set before their eyes than the example of a godly, Christian married couple. It is always good to involve parents and other mature lay people in the youth ministry. Parents are the real professionals when it comes to youth work. They should have the opportunity to minister to young people outside of their own home.

O-VERSEE EACH SPECIFIC AREA OF MINISTRY

It is necessary to delegate responsibility to workers, but it is more important not to relinquish leadership. The workers should always be accountable to the leader. Check up on responsibilities and assignments that have been delegated. Make sure things are being done the right way. Sometimes it is necessary to hold their feet to the fire to maintain Christ-honoring leadership.

R-ESERVE THE RIGHT TO MOVE WORKERS AROUND FOR GREATER EFFECTIVENESS

Workers need to serve in different aspects of the youth ministry to see the overall picture. This will keep them from becoming apathetic and stagnant. When a worker feels like "this is my ministry and I'll do it the way I want," you have a real problem to fix. Every worker should feel some measure of personal responsibility.

However when a youth worker becomes unteachable and unchangeable, it is time to move them to another area of responsibility.

K-NOW THEIR WEAKNESSES AND SEEK TO PATIENTLY BRING THEM ALONG

Everyone has weaknesses. These will most certainly become magnified when you begin to work with teenagers. When you discover an undesirable trait in one of your workers, do not give up on them too soon. Many times problems can be fixed by praying them through it, talking to them about it, or training them out of it. Exercise patience with workers and ask them to do the same with you. With a little investment of time, these people can become our greatest assests in the ministry.

E-NCOURAGE WORKERS OFTEN

Youth leaders should always remember to show appreciation to those who serve as workers. Build a special rapport with those under your leadership. Write them letters, speak with them privately, and praise them publicly. When things go well, give them the credit for it. *"Withhold not good from them to whom it is due, when it is in the power of thine hand to do it"* (Proverbs 3:27).

R-equire Faithfulness on the Part of All Youth Workers

The youth worker must be willing to pay the price of faithfulness in the Christian life. Encourage them to be faithful in giving, church attendance, soulwinning, Bible study, and prayer. These five areas should be mandatory for all workers in youth ministry.

S-eek The Advice and Input of youth workers on a Regular Basis

Many great ideas come from insightful workers. Discuss future activities together. Learn to use good ideas, even when they did not originate with the you. Workers are often turned off to the "one man show." Allow them to give input on important decisions. It will make them feel as though they are part of the ultimate success or failure of the program.

SETTING THE FOUNDATION

The foundation work is the most crucial stage of construction. Nothing can be built until the foundation is laid. Although no one usually notices the foundation of a building, it provides the strength for the overall structure. In order for the building to stand the test of time, someone must take cautious care when laying the foundation. This important work cannot be appproached with negligence. You can fix many things down the road, but you cannot rebuild the foundation.

In the work of the Lord, the true foundation is the Lord Jesus Christ. I Corinthians 3:11 says, *"For other foundation can no man lay than that is laid, which is Jesus Christ."* Jesus said in Luke 6:46-48, *"And why call ye me, Lord, Lord, and do not the things which I say? Whosoever cometh to me, and heareth my sayings, and doeth them, I will shew you to whom he is like: He is like a man which built an house, and digged deep, and laid the foundation on a rock: and when the flood arose, the stream beat vehemently upon that house, and could not shake it: for it was founded upon a rock."*

The stability of a Christ-honoring youth ministry can be traced back to a solid foundation. The local church youth ministry must have foundational principles upon which it is built. Many youth ministries never survive the storms of life because the foundation was not properly laid. May God help us to take cautious care in building a large and sure foundation for the glory of the Lord and for the sake of young people.

CHAPTER 10

DEVELOPING THE RIGHT PHILOSOPHY

Our philosophy of youth ministry is important. If building a biblical youth ministry is our goal, then we must make sure we have the proper philosophy concerning youth work. Behind every deliberate action, there is a philosophy. Our philosophy will determine the course of action we

> Behind every deliberate action, there is a philosophy.

take in working with teenagers. Our philosophy tells us what we believe; what we believe determines our actions, and our actions determine our outcome. Therefore, it is imperative that our philosophy springs forth from the Word of God.

Every youth leader's philosophy is being or has been molded by three factors in their life:

1. **The ministries to which they are exposed**
2. **The books they have read**
3. **The people with whom they are associated**

SECULAR PHILOSOPHIES OF YOUTH MINISTRY

There are four secular philosophies of youth ministry that we should avoid. A secular philosophy, when developed and practiced, will provide for the *temporary* but not for the *eternal*.

1. "Keeping Kids Off the Street"

This philosophy holds to the idea that if we can keep teenagers off the streets, we will be able to keep them out of trouble. So, gymnasiums are built and anyone and everyone are brought in with the hope that a Christian environment will change behavior. If a pig is taken out of a pigpen, bathed and sprayed with perfume, he may act civilized for a moment, but when given the opportunity, he will return to the slop from which he came. It is his nature to do so. Likewise, teenagers have a sinful nature. This is why there are gangs, violence, crime, and vagrancy in our neighborhoods. Our philosophy should not be "Let's keep them off the streets." It should be "Let's keep them out of hell!" Our goal is not to get them out of the world, but to get worldliness out of them.

2. "Be Like Them in Order to Reach Them"

Some youth ministers, in an effort to build rapport with teenagers, will adopt their dress, hairstyles, speech, and attitudes. This is not wise. Using teen vernacular will only cause disrespect in the long run. Jesus ministered to publicans, Pharisees, and sinners without ever becoming one. We cannot get into the ditch with them in order to reach them. Someone must stand on solid ground in order to truly help a troubled teenager. II Corinthians 6:17 says, *"...Come out from among them, and be ye separate..."*

3. "Entertain Them - Keep them Busy"

This secular philosophy is the over-emphasis of entertainment. It is believed that if teens are not entertained, they will not faithfully attend the church. So, the youth leader wears himself to a frazzle with an afterglow on Sunday night, putt-putt golf on Monday night, bowling on Tuesday, Pizza Hut after church on Wednesday, skating on Thursday, movie night on Friday and a car wash on Saturday. In an effort to keep teens busy, he has neglected his own wife, family, and other important areas of his ministry. In essence, he has become a "spiritual baby-sitter," providing much activity, but little spiritual progress in the lives of young people.

Activities are fun and necessary in their proper place of priority. However, if the driving force of our youth ministry is entertainment, then we have developed a secular philosophy and not a scriptural one.

4. "Large Numbers Equal Success"

It is very easy to get caught up in the "numbers game." Some of the largest youth ministries in the country exist in the midst of churches that are preaching and teaching false doctrine and host worldly worship. Some are even cults. If we are averaging thirty teens in Sunday school, and the church across town is averaging ninety, we then feel that we have failed the Lord. To equate success to largeness is often deceiving.

An evangelist told the story of traveling to preach at a week-long revival. As he traveled on Monday, a dog crossed the road and was struck by his vehicle. He noticed that the dog fell on the side of the road and died. As he traveled back on Friday, he noticed the dog was still lying there, except it was larger on Friday than it was on Monday! Some would say the dog was growing, but actually, it was swelling. It was so full of corruption that it swelled and gave the appearance of growth and life, but actually, it was dead. Not every large youth group is growing because of God's blessing. Some are

> God does not measure success by numbers, programs, or a balanced budget.

successfully swelling because of the corruption and worldliness on the inside.

God does not measure success by numbers, programs or a balanced budget. He measures success by the youth leader's faithful obedience and by the extent to which he does all things to God's glory. We must remember that at the Judgment Seat of Christ, every man's work will be tried by what *sort* it is, not by what *size* it is. In the eyes of God, sort is more important than size. If the sort is right, God will give the increase and growth will be inevitable. I Corinthians 3:13 says, ***"Every man's work shall be made manifest: for the day shall declare it, because it shall be revealed by fire; and the fire shall try every man's work of what sort it is."***

99

SCRIPTURAL PHILOSOPHIES OF YOUTH MINISTRY

The Biblical youth ministry should be built upon philosophies that are obtained from the truths of God's Word. There are six essential philosophies that should lay the groundwork for our ministry to teenagers.

1. The youth ministry must be over-seen by the local church pastor

"Remember them which have the rule over you, who have spoken unto you the word of God: whose faith follow, considering the end of their conversation. Obey them that have the rule over you, and submit yourselves: for they watch for your souls, as they that must give account, that they may do it with joy, and not with grief: for that is unprofitable for you." (Hebrews 13:7,17)

God has ordained the pastor as the undershepherd and overseer of the New Testament church. He is ultimately responsible to God for every ministry of the local church and will give an account to God at the Judgment Seat of Christ. As he takes the oversight thereof, God will give him wisdom and direction for the church. With this thought in mind, we understand that the youth ministry is to be inclusive and not to be exclusive of itself. It does not stand alone, but it works together with other ministries of the same body. The pastor has an understanding of how these ministries work together to edify the whole church. As the overseer, he must choose or approve the leadership in the youth ministry. This may include hiring a youth director or selecting those to teach youth classes or supervise youth activities. No one has a greater burden for teenagers than the local church pastor.

2. The youth director must be an extention of the pastor's ministry

"And he gave some, apostles; and some, prophets; and some, evangelists; and some, pastors and teachers; For the perfecting of the saints, for the work of the ministry, for the edifying of the body of Christ:" (Ephesians 4:11-12)

> The primary role of the youth director is to be an extention of the ministry of the pastor to the teenagers.

We sometimes use the title "youth pastor," but in a truer sense, we should say "youth director" or "youth leader" because there is only one pastor of a New Testament church. The primary role of the youth director is to be an extention of the ministry of the pastor to the teenagers. He is to point them to pastoral authority as he leads them in the Christian life. A youth leader must take the time to learn the burden and vision of the pastor, and he should share the same philosophy with the pastor concerning helping young people. He is to keep an open line of communication with the pastor by informing him of any plans, activities, programs, or counseling made to young people. He must always remember that this position of leadership has been given to him by the pastor.

3. The youth ministry must strengthen the Christian home

"And he shall go before him in the spirit and power of Elias, to turn the hearts of the fathers to the children, and the disobedient to the wisdom of the just; to make ready a people prepared for the Lord." (Luke 1:17)

God has ordained two institutions that will influence the teenager for the rest of their lives: the Christian home and the local church. Long after the teenager leaves the youth ministry, these two institutions will be there to guide and minister to young people. The first great priority when helping Christian young people is to seek to minister to the entire family. As stated previously, the local church youth ministry should not *compete* with the home; it should *complement* the home. Successful youth ministry is more than just *instructing* the teenager; it is *involving* the parent. The youth ministry that seeks to isolate the teenager from their parents and siblings is destructive. The youth director should never be a substitute for the parent. Teenagers need to be turned to the God-given authority of their parents. The greatest achievement in youth ministry is when the parent/teen relationship has been strengthened and helped.

> Successful youth ministry is more than just *instructing* the teenager; it is *involving* the parent.

4. The youth ministry must tie the teen to the local church

"Husbands, love your wives, even as Christ also loved the church, and gave himself for it;" (Ephesians 5:25)

The greatest work of God is accomplished through the ministry of the local, New Testament church. The greatest failure in youth work is the neglect to tie the teenager to the ministry of the local church and to the authority of the pastor. As a result, a vast majority of young people are no longer involved in church after they graduate. Many youth directors take a short-sighted look at the youth ministry, seeing only from the 7th through the 12th grade years. Many times teenagers graduate from high school and feel disconnected from the church. This happens when the youth director endears the teenager to himself instead of to the ministry of the local church.

5. The youth ministry must be larger than the youth group

The local church youth ministry must not only minister to young people but also *through* young people.

"*And Jesus, when he came out, saw much people, and was moved with compassion toward them, because they were as sheep not having a shepherd: and he began to teach them many things.*" (Mark 6:34)

Many times we fall into the trap of focusing on the youth group instead of on the youth ministry. The expression "youth group" has a tendency to turn everything inward. If we are not careful, we will create a "holy huddle" that excludes the outreach of new teenagers. The end result is a stagnant youth program. The local church youth ministry must not only minister *to* young people but also *through* young people. Using the expression "youth ministry" will help us to turn everything outward. This is the Biblical viewpoint God wants us to have. Jesus not only saw the disciples, but He saw the multitude. May our Lord help us to see a bigger picture.

6. The youth ministry will reap a harvest where the emphasis is placed

"Be not deceived; God is not mocked: for whatsoever a man soweth, that shall he also reap." (Galatians 6:7)

In most youth ministries, the emphasis has been on entertainment: super activities, big parties, special trips, and fun games. It does not take long for the youth director to realize that church entertainment can never compete with the world's entertainment, and it should not seek to do so. If this becomes our emphasis, it will produce a group of spoiled teenagers who have to be constantly pampered and entertained with the latest gimic to keep their interest. We need to remember this great philosophy: *You always reap a harvest where you place the emphasis.* If our youth ministries are striving to produce exemplary teenagers with a heart for God, it will not happen by accident. We must be busy emphasizing the right things with our young people. A helpful checklist might include:

- Am I emphasizing the obedient Christian life?
- Am I emphasizing full-time Christian service?
- Am I emphasizing the responsibility to win the lost?
- Am I emphasizing strong standards and convictions?
- Am I emphasizing the surrendered life?
- Am I emphasizing the need of gospel preachers and missionaries for the next generation?
- Am I emphasizing future Bible college education?
- Am I emphasizing the authority of the Bible in our life?
- Am I emphasizing faithfulness to the Lord and to the local church?

These Biblical philosophies must be ingrained in our thinking and practiced in our ministry. If we wish to see young people come through the youth ministry with a heart for God and a desire to serve him with their life. We must have the right philosophy if we are to produce the right product for the glory of God.

CHAPTER 11

DEFINING THE RIGHT PURPOSE

There are many youth leaders who are busy conducting programs and activities, but they cannot state the Biblical purpose behind what they are doing. In the absence of a Biblical purpose, there is little chance of developing a productive youth ministry. Strong youth ministries are not built on programs, personalities, or gimmicks. They are built on the eternal purposes of God.

A purpose statement should be developed for the youth ministry. This stated purpose will answer the question of *why* your youth ministry exists. When there is no clear communication about *why* and *what* you are doing, people get frustrated. The youth ministry with no purposeful direction will produce youth workers who feel that their work in the youth ministry is not important.

There is a six-fold purpose that will keep us on track in the local church youth ministry.

1. SALVATION - *Telling* teenagers the messsage of the gospel of Jesus Christ

"And he said unto them, Go ye into all the world, and preach the gospel to every creature." (Mark 16:15)

God's great plan and purpose for young people begins at Calvary. Until there is an experience of salvation, all other goals are secondary. Every lure we use to attract young people should have the gospel hook attatched to it. Every program should seek to win the lost to Christ. The first question we should ask ourselves when meeting a new teenager should be, "Is this young person a Christian?" George W. Truett once said, "The bringing of one soul to Jesus is the highest achievement possible to human life."

> Every lure we use to attract young people should have the gospel hook attatched to it.

After salvation, we must not forget to teach them to follow the Lord Jesus in believer's baptism. Matthew 28:19 says, *"Go ye therefore, and teach all nations, baptizing them in the name of the Father, and of the Son, and of the Holy Ghost."* This step of obedience will bring the blessing and favor of God upon their lives. If we really want God's best for teenagers, then we must purpose to see them saved and baptized.

2. SCRIPTURE STUDY - *Teaching* teenagers the principles and doctrines of the Word of God

"Teaching them to observe all things whatsoever I have commanded you: and, lo, I am with you alway, even unto the end of the world. Amen." (Matthew 28:20)

Along with salvation and baptism, the work of discipleship is also a part of the Great Commission. After the teenager has been won to Christ, we must begin to systematically teach him *"all things"* of the Bible. Teenagers need to be grounded in the truths of God's Word. Every teenager in our ministry should be plugged into a Sunday School class or new converts' class that will begin to introduce them to the doctrinal truths, principles, and characters of the Bible. We must teach them that the Bible is to be established as the final authority in their Christian life for faith and practice.

3. SURRENDER - *Turning* teenagers from self-centeredness to Christ-centeredness

"I beseech you therefore, brethren, by the

mercies of God, that ye present your bodies a living sacrifice, holy, acceptable unto God, which is your reasonable service."
(Romans 12:1)

The human nature of all young people says, "Look out for number one." Early in the Christian life, teenagers should be challenged to yield their life and ambitions to Christ, seeking to please Him and not themselves. They must learn that the secret of the Christian life is surrender. Every battle in the Christian life can be won through surrender! Pride and self-centeredness are two peculiar sins of youth. Pride is the oldest sin in the world and has ruined the lives of young people through every generation since Adam. It is dangerous because it makes us think that we are good enough as we are and causes us to be satisfied with ourselves. This is why in Proverbs 6:16-17 the *"proud look"* is at the very top of God's hate list. When young people become truly surrendered to the Lord, they will seek to serve others more than themselves. They will place God's plan and purpose above their own.

> Pride and self-centeredness are two peculiar sins of youth.

4. SERVICE - *Tying* teenagers to the fellowship and ministry of the local church

"But if we walk in the light, as he is in the light, we have fellowship one with another, and the blood of Jesus Christ his Son cleanseth us from all sin." (I John 1:7)

God did not intend for Christians to live in solitude. He desires us to be identified with the body of Christ and to enjoy the fellowship of other believers. There is no subsitute for the fellowship of the local church. Christian young people should not have to look elsewhere for encouragement and a sense of belonging. In this local fellowship of believers, the teenager should find a variety of ministries in which they can serve the Lord. The happiest, most fulfilled young people in our church are those who have found their place of Christian service. We have learned that if they do not feel a *part of* it, they will eventually *depart from* it. Dedicated young people should always be moving forward in development for Christian service.

> We have learned that if they do not feel a *part of* it, they will eventually *depart from* it.

5. SOUL WINNING - *Training* teenagers to tell others of their faith in Christ

"And he gave some, apostles; and some, prophets; and some, evangelists; and some, pastors and teachers; For the perfecting of the saints, for the work of the ministry, for the edifying of the body of Christ:" (Ephesians 4:11-12)

It is our responsibility to lead teens to Christ and to teach them to tell others. Preparation for a lifetime of Christian service should be initiated as early as possible with teenagers. Our goal is not to *entertain* them but to *equip* them to serve the Lord Jesus with their life.

In most churches, we have unintentionally cultivated at least three heresies about teenagers:

Heresy #1 - *Teenagers do not have the ability to be effective -exemplary Christians.*

Heresy #2 - *Teenagers cannot be counted upon for any type of productive ministry.*

Heresy #3 -*Teenagers are the church of tomorrow.*

It is time for us to lay these heresies aside and to challenge our young people to stand strong and speak boldly for Jesus Christ. The truth is that teenagers, when given the opportunity, will rise to the occasion if properly equipped for Christian service and soul winning. Christian young people need to know how to share their personal testimony and how to share the gospel plan of salvation. Much of their time at church is wasted while sitting on car hoods before and after the services. It is advantageous for us to use every available minute with teens to teach and train them for the ministry, especially while they are on the church property.

6. SEPARATION - *Transforming* teenagers from worldliness to the likeness of Christ

"And be not conformed to this world: but be ye transformed by the renewing of your mind, that ye may prove what is that good, and acceptable, and perfect, will of God." (Romans 12:2)

Biblical separation is not an *immediate* work, nor is it a

> There can always be found a remnant of Christian young people who are willing to separate their lives unto holiness.

final work in the life of the believer. It is a *progressive* work that will not end until we receive our glorified body. When sincere young people begin to seek the Lord, they will have a desire to separate themselves from the world. We see an illustration of this in the life of Josiah. When he was 16 years old, he began to seek after God. Josiah practiced biblical separation. (II Chronicles 34:1-3) As soon as he began seeking God, he began to destroy the idolatry in Judah. He began to purge the land of sin and corruption.

There can always be found a remnant of Christian young people who are willing to separate their lives unto holiness. This is not an easy road in the Christian life. It is the high road. Christian young people can find great joy in a life that is separated from the world and unto the Lord. Someone must instruct them how to lay aside the weights and sins that will beset them in their walk with Christ. As young people are transformed to the image of Christ, they will have a more effective testimony as they seek to share the gospel with others.

These six purposes - *salvation, scripture study, surrender, service, soul winning,* and *separation* - should guide our thinking as we seek to help every teenager through the days of their youth.

CHAPTER 12

DETERMINING THE RIGHT PROGRAMS

The right philosophy and purpose will answer the question of "why" in the youth ministry. The right programs will answer the question of "how" you will accomplish your purpose. Programs are the vehicle used to carry out your purpose. A biblical program for the youth ministry should be geared to produce a well balanced Christian who is ready to face the challenges of life and should help accomplish the six purposes of youth ministry.

> Programs are the vehicle used to carry out your purpose.

Achieving proper balance in this area will be a constant challenge for the youth leader. This is where accountability to the pastor becomes crucial. Seek his advice. As the overseer of the flock, the pastor can advise you when your programs have gotten out of balance. There is a great temptation to become too weak in one area and too strong in another. Having the pastor's approval upon the programs you have chosen will eliminate a lot of frustration in the ministry.

There are many good programs that are available for the youth ministry today. Do what is best for your church.

USE PROGRAMS TO PROMOTE EVANGELISM

> Evangelism is not a program—it is a pattern of life.

Evangelism is not a program; it is a pattern of life. Christian teenagers should catch the spirit of evangelism through the local church. Young people will have more opportunities to witness for Christ in their daily routine than adults will. They should personally feel a burden to reach the lost for Christ.

Even though evangelism itself is not a program, there are programs that encourage evangelism.

- **The Evangelistic Youth Activity**
  Teens should be using social activities as a point of contact and an opportunity to invite their unsaved friends with the ultimate purpose of winning those friends to Christ. Several times throughout the year, an evangelistic activity can be used to bring in the unsaved to hear the gospel of salvation. Whether it is a youth rally,

evangelistic film, lock-in, teen conference, or pizza blast, always make an appeal for salvation.

- **The Evangelistic Sunday School**
  The teen Sunday School class does more than just teach the Bible. It places an emphasis on reaching new people. The evangelistic Sunday School makes much use of campaigns and special days. A few examples are "Roundup Day," "Friend Sunday," "Each One Reach One Sunday" and "Double Attendance Day." Promoting evangelism through the Sunday School will increase attendance, add to the enrollment, build excitement, reach new people, and emphasize soul winning.

- **The Teen Soul-Winning Program**
  Every church should have a designated time when teens meet together for the purpose of sharing the gospel. This door-to-door visitation program can be conducted before the midweek service or on Saturday afternoon. Host a special training class that equips teenagers to be more effective in their witnessing.

USE PROGRAMS TO PROMOTE DISCIPLESHIP

True discipleship is simply helping teens become more like Christ. The Bible says, *"And Jesus increased in wisdom and stature, and in favour with God and man"* (Luke 2:52). When teenagers are discipled, they begin to grow in every area of the Christian life.

- **Bible Studies**
  Teaching young people about Bible characters, doctrines, and principles are important.

- **Teen Leadership Training**
  Have a class that teaches leadership qualities and Christian character traits. Teens should also be trained in the area of soul winning in this program.

- **New Converts Class**
  This program is for those who are new Christians. Encourage those young people how to be a 5-Star Christian: read the Bible, pray, witness, be faithful to church and give.

- **Timothy Club**
  This discipleship program is just for young men, teaching them how to be a godly man, how to be a

spiritual leader, how to take outlines, how to preach or teach and how to overcome temptation, etc.

- **Christian Charm Class**
  This discipleship program is for young ladies. The youth director's wife or pastor's wife can teach on how to be a godly wife, proper etiquette, how to set a table, how to dress, and what to look for in a husband, etc.

USE PROGRAMS TO PROMOTE FELLOWSHIP

Christian teenagers love to spend time together. Special times should be planned to provide fellowship for the committed teenagers in the church, those who attend faithfully the services, and those who are serving in the ministry.

- **Retreats**
  Retreats provide an excellent time of fellowship for the youth group. Have great food, have a lot of recreation, and keep the cost low. A good time to have a retreat with your teens is in the winter, four to six months after they have been to camp. This is the youth leader's opportunity to challenge teens that may have slipped away from their

commitments. Share your vision and goals for the youth ministry for the upcoming year. Endear new teenagers to yourself and to the youth group.

- **Banquets**

  A teen banquet is a special activity that everyone will enjoy. Banquets can be used for fellowship several times throughout the year. Have a Valentine Banquet in February, a Junior/Senior Banquet in May, a Christmas Banquet in December, or for an added twist, a "Crazy Banquet" with fun games, surprising skits, silliness, and a theme for casual dress.

- **Summer Teen Camp**

  Summer camp is not an evangelistic tool of the youth ministry. Some teens may get the assurance of their salvation at camp, but it is not wise to knowingly enlist unsaved teens for camp. You will find yourself dealing with problems instead of helping your key teenagers. Unsaved teens can be reached through the local church and Sunday School. Teen camp should be a week of fellowship and challenge for the committed teens in your church. Spiritual progress should be made with the entire group. Summer camp brings young people together like no other event. Spiritual commitments and decisions are made that will last a lifetime.

USE PROGRAMS TO PROMOTE WORSHIP AND CHRISTIAN SERVICE

Christian teenagers need to express themselves through worship and ministry opportunities. Teenagers at all age levels can fulfill the purpose of worshipping and serving Christ through the various ministries of the local church, such as Vacation Bible School, teen mission trips, teen choirs and ensembles, the bus ministry, junior church, etc.

- **Teen Choir**
  Music is the most effective vehicle for preparing hearts to receive the Word of God. Have a weekly practice time for the teen choir or ensemble. Adequate preparation and practice is an essential requirement for every performance. Sing uplifting music that will bring their hearts close to God. Much of our worship is expressed through singing. Ephesians 5:19 says, ***"Speaking to yourselves in psalms and hymns and spiritual songs, singing and making melody in your heart to the Lord."***

- **Ushers and Greeters**
  Encourage young people to dress sharply and appropriately for the worship services. Allow some of these young people to serve as ushers and greeters. Taking the offering, passing out bulletins, holding the door for people, or shaking hands with a warm, smiling face can certainly enhance the worship service of any church.

- **Teen Mission Trips**
  There are many churches that have never taken teenagers to the mission field. The summer mission trip will introduce young people to the life and ministry of the local church missionary. This is one of the most life-changing experiences that young people could ever witness. When teenagers see the living conditions in many foreign countries, they become much more appreciative of their own circumstances. Their hearts will be stirred over the multitude of people who have never heard the gospel in their own language. On many occasions, the Lord will use such a trip to call labourers into His harvest.

- **Evangelistic Bus Ministry**
  There is a resurgence across America of churches that see the need and opportunity to evangelize neighborhoods through the bus ministry. It is

thrilling to see young people at the Saturday bus meeting as they make ready to visit the bus routes through door-to-door visitation. God will give them a burden for the lost as they go into all the world, focusing on our "Jerusalem."

• **Vacation Bible School**
The first VBS was conducted in 1898 by Mrs. Walker Aylett. Hanes, a Sunday school teacher at Ephiphany Baptist Church in New York.[15] Her desire was to reach out to the neglected children on the east side of New York. This week-long evangelistic meeting has seen thousands of children saved over the last decade. The VBS program affords the teenager an opportunity to minister to children in a variety of ways. There are classes to be taught, refreshments to be served, crafts to be built, and children to be brought to Christ. Teenagers can be encouraged to serve the Lord by giving them a small assignment in the summer VBS program.

   Be responsible to make sure that all programs are Biblically based and Pastor-approved!

STRENGTHENING THE WALLS

Walls are established for security and protection from predators without, while offering safety to those within. A structure with no walls becomes an easy prey to vandalism and invaders. A structure must also be properly walled in order to weather the storms that will threaten the work of construction.

In this day and age, people are talking much about "tearing down the walls." Although they are referring to the walls of hatred, racism, and indifference, the idea has carried over to other areas of life. In the Biblical youth ministry, walls must be established in the life of a teenager, not torn down. Some of these walls already exist and must therefore be strengthened.

Satan would love to tear down the walls that protect the teenager in life's journey. When these walls are broken down, there is no resistance against the vandal from hell. He is roaming about, as a roaring lion, seeking someone to devour (I Peter 5:8). When permanent walls surround a teenager, they can weather the storms of life and remain unharmed by the wicked one. Isaiah 49:16

says, **"Behold, I have graven thee upon the palms of my hands; thy walls are continually before me."**

CHAPTER 13

THE WALL OF PARENTAL AUTHORITY

A wise youth leader will come to the conclusion that parents are not the enemies of the youth ministry; they are the allies. A family-friendly youth ministry is vital. When you have the support of parents, half of your battle is already won. Trying to have a ministry to teenagers that excludes parents is about as effective as a Band-Aid on a hemorrhage. The church and the youth leader are to help the parents to perform their God-ordained role of building a unified home in which to train their children for God.

Many parents are apathetic toward, feel threatened by, or are resentful of the youth ministry. These obstacles can be overcome by gaining the parents' confidence and by helping them to see their responsibilities to the youth ministry and to their own teenager.

Tying the family and youth ministry together takes time. Many parents want to be helpful and supportive of the youth ministry but do not know how. There are three "Be-attitudes" parents can learn:

1. Be Committed

Parents should support the youth leadership in the church and should be informed of the dangers of criticizing leadership in the home. They must be taught that they should never discuss disagreements they have with spiritual leadership in front of the teenager. The parent should be encouraged to pray for the youth ministry, that God might grant wisdom and spiritual discernment to its leadership.

2. Be Concerned

Parents should be concerned about the spiritual growth of your teenager. Deuteronomy 6:5-7, *"And thou shalt love the LORD thy God with all thine heart, and with all thy soul, and with all thy might. And these words, which I command thee this day, shall be in thine heart: And thou shalt teach them diligently unto thy children, and shalt talk of them when thou sittest in thine house, and when thou walkest by the way, and when thou liest down, and when thou risest up."* These verses teach that parents must monitor the spiritual growth of their own children, asking themselves "Is my teenager winning souls, reading their Bible, praying, giving, obeying at home and school?" Any concern on the part of the parent should be openly discussed with the youth leadership. Encourage parents to communicate with you. The parent and youth leader should both desire the same goal for the teenager- spiritual progress and Christlikeness.

3. Be Counted On

Parents should be counted on for participation and involvement. Inviting parents to help with activities, programs, and trips can be one of the wisest moves you make as a youth leader. If the right parents are enlisted, a new level of support and enthusiasm will invade the youth ministry. A worthy goal of the youth director should be to keep families *involved* (participation), *informed* (communication), and *inspired* (inspiration).

A recent survey revealed that teenage alienation from religion is highly correlated with a poor relationship between teens and their parents.[16] The home environment must be a living example of real Christianity in action and not one that pays mere lip service. Parents have a four-fold responsibility to the teenager in their home.

1. GUIDE THEIR STEPS IN THE LORD

> Parents must accept the responsibility of guiding the teenager *"in the way he should go."*

Proverbs 22:6 says, *"Train up a child in the way he should go: and when he is old, he will not depart from it."* Proverbs 29:16 says, *"When the wicked are multiplied, transgression increaseth: but the righteous shall see their fall."* In the average home, the job of parenting is left up to the teenager; not to the parents. The Christian home should be different. Parents must accept the responsibility of guiding the teenager *"in the way he should go."* Spiritual decisions should not be left entirely up to the teenager. Just as the teen is instructed to take a bath, brush his teeth, and go to bed at a certain hour, the teenager should also be instructed to be faithful to church, have the right friendships, and make the right decisions. This is not *forcing* religion upon the teenager, this is *guiding* the teen to make spiritual decisions. When they are old, they will not depart from it.

2. GUARD THEIR HEART AND LIFE FROM EVIL

Proverbs 4:23 says, *"Keep thy heart with all diligence; for out of it are the issues of life."*

- **Their *affections* should be guarded.**

  I John 2:15 says, *"Love not the world, neither the things that are in the world. If any man love the world, the love of the Father is not in him."* It has been said that our affection determines our direction. Be careful of what you allow your teenager to fall in love with. What they give their heart to is what they will love. Encourage them to set their affections on things above.

- **Their *actions* should be guarded.**

  John 8:29 says, *"And he that sent me is with me: the Father hath not left me alone; for I do always those things that please him."* When a teenager is permitted to take a job on Sundays or on Wednesday nights, or to play a sport that requires them to miss church, it is injurious to their spiritual well-being. The parent should carefully guard what the teenager does, where they go, and in what they get involved. Proverbs 3:6 reminds us, *"In all thy ways acknowledge him..."*

- **Their *associates* should be guarded.**

Proverbs 13:20 says, *"He that walketh with wise men shall be wise: but a companion of fools shall be destroyed."* Nothing can be more detrimental to a Christian teenager than the friends with which they are allowed to associate. In most cases, teens are not wise in choosing the right type of friends. They need guidance. Steering a teenager away from the wrong influences will take grace and tactfulness. The wise parent must look down the road and break up some relationships *before* they become strong. A Biblical standard for dating or friendships would be found in II Corinthians 6:14: *"Be ye not unequally yoked together with unbelievers: for what fellowship hath righteousness with unrighteousness? and what communion hath light with darkness?"*

- **Their *appearance* should be guarded.**
  I Samuel 16:7 says, *"But the LORD said unto Samuel, Look not on his countenance, or on the height of his stature; because I have refused him: for the LORD seeth not as man seeth; for man looketh on the outward appearance,*

but the LORD looketh on the heart." Maintaining a good testimony in our appearance is important because *"man looketh on the outward appearance."* The goal of setting dress standards is to avoid that which offends morally. Immodest apparel is forbidden in the Bible. Biblical

> When the *heart-line* is right, the *hair-line* and *hem-line* will be right too!

dress standards can be guided by at least three scripture passages:

I Timothy 2:9, *"In like manner also, that women adorn themselves in modest apparel, with shamefacedness and sobriety; not with broided hair, or gold, or pearls, or costly array."* (This verse emphasizes modesty or not drawing attention to the body.)

I John 2:15-17, *"Love not the world, neither the things that are in the world. If any man love the world, the love of the Father is not in him. For all that is in the world, the lust of the flesh, and the lust of the eyes, and the pride of life,*

*is not of the Father, but is of the world.
And the world passeth away, and the lust
thereof: but he that doeth the will of God
abideth forever. "* (These verses instruct
us not to imitate the world)

II Timothy 2:22, *"Flee also
youthful lusts: but follow righteousness,
faith, charity, peace, with them that call
on the Lord out of a pure heart."* Romans
*14:13, "Let us not therefore judge one
another any more: but judge this rather,
that no man put a stumblingblock or an
occasion to fall in his brother's way."*
(These verses caution the young person
about how his dress may affect another
believer.)

How the teenager dresses and looks
will communicate to others what is really
in his heart. The Christian teenager should
be steered away from an appearance that is
sloppy, sensual, sexual, or fashioned after
the fads of the world. Parents should
encourage an appearance that is sharp, neat,
appropriate and modest - all of which are
always in style. The key to winning the
victory in this area is having a heart that is

right with God. When the *heart-line* is right, the *hair-line* and *hem-line* will be right too!

3. GROUND THEM IN THE WORD OF GOD

Isaiah 38:19 says, *"The living, the living, he shall praise thee, as I do this day: the father to the children shall make known thy truth."* Isaiah 28:9 asks, *"Whom shall he teach knowledge? and whom shall he make to understand doctrine? them that are weaned from the milk, and drawn from the breasts."* It is not the primary responsibility of the church to teach Biblical truth to young people. This responsibility is afforded to the parent. The authority of the Bible must be established in the home. Maintain the family altar of devotions and prayer. J. Edgar Hoover said, "Juvenile delinquency is not cured in the electric chair, but in the high chair." Teenagers should find truth at home to help them overcome the temptations of the world. The youth leader's role in a teenager's spiritual development is helpful, but a parent's role is crucial.

4. GLEAN WISDOM FROM OTHERS

Proverbs 13:20 tells us, *"He that walketh with wise men shall be wise: but a companion of fools shall be destroyed.* " Parents find it encouraging when they realize they are not alone in their situation. There are other parents in the church who have had success in raising teenagers. The wise parent should never feel awkward about seeking the advice of the pastor, deacons, or any other person in the church who could give sound advice on rearing teens. This is not a sign of *weakness*; it is a sign of *wisdom.* Proverbs 24:6 says, *"For by wise counsel thou shalt make thy war: and in multitude of counsellors there is safety. "*

The wall of parental authority is not fortified for the purpose of limiting freedom, but for the God-given purpose of protection and security. Neither the teenager nor the youth director must ever violate the parental authority God has established in life. This wall should consistently be strengthened by the youth ministry. The parents are the final authority in the life of the teenager, and we are wrong when we do not respect this authority. Teenagers should lean on the wall of parental authority until they reach an age of maturity where they can make wise decisions and step out into a life of adult responsibility.

CHAPTER 14

THE WALL OF SPIRITUAL LEADERSHIP

Hebrews 13:7 & 17 say, *"Remember them which have the rule over you, who have spoken unto you the word of God: whose faith follow, considering the end of their conversation." "Obey them that have the rule over you, and submit yourselves: for they watch for your souls, as they that must give account, that they may do it with joy, and not with grief: for that is unprofitable for you."* According to the Bible, God has given to us the protection and privilege of spiritual leadership. There will come a day in the life of the teenager when they will need the help of godly leadership for advice and counsel. This spiritual leadership may consist of a parent, faithful youth director, Sunday school teacher, pastor, deacon, youth worker, or wise adult layman in the church. This wall of spiritual leadership must remain strong in the teenager's life.

One mistake that many parents make is openly criticizing spiritual leadership in their home. Undoubtedly, leadership will not always be right. However, when there is a disagreement or conflict, it should never be discussed with the teenager. When this happens, a wall is being broken down that God established for protection in the teenager's life. Parents should learn never to criticize or undermine other authority figures in their child's life. They should back up their teachers, principal, youth pastor, and especially their pastor. They should know that if children are allowed to criticize their spiritual leaders when they are not around, they will also criticize their parents when they are not around.

Once a teenager loses respect for a spiritual leader, it is hardly ever regained. Sometimes the parent is the cause of this tragedy. In our homes we would be wise to follow Ephesians 4:29 which says, *"Let no corrupt communication proceed out of your mouth, but that which is good to the use of edifying, that it may minister grace unto the hearers."*

How can a parent and teenager strengthen the wall of spiritual leadership?

PRAY FOR SPIRITUAL LEADERSHIP

I Timothy 2:1-2 says, *"I exhort therefore, that, first of all, supplications, prayers, intercessions, and giving of thanks, be made for all men; For kings, and for all that are in authority; that we may lead a quiet and peaceable life in all godliness and honesty."* God's Word instructs us to pray for all those that have authority in our lives. When we criticize leadership more than we pray for leadership, we have violated the Word of God. Teenagers should hear their parents pray for the pastor, youth pastor, Sunday school teacher, etc. in their home on a regular basis.

PROMOTE SPIRITUAL LEADERSHIP

Romans 13:7 says, *"Render therefore to all their dues: tribute to whom tribute is due; custom to whom custom; fear to whom fear; honour to whom honour."* I Timothy 5:17 says, *"Let the elders that rule well be counted worthy of double honour, especially they who labour in the word and doctrine."* A spiritual leader is not to be the recipient of worship, but he is to be honoured. When we teach our young people to honour the man of God, we are promoting leadership in their lives. Parents should encourage their children to seek the advice of the pastor or youth leaders God has given them. When properly promoted, young people will hold a pastor in the highest regard because of the work God has given them to do.

BE PATIENT WITH SPIRITUAL LEADERSHIP

I Thessalonians 5:14 says, *"Now we exhort you, brethren, warn them that are unruly, comfort the feebleminded, support the weak, be patient toward all men."* It is amazing how we as Christians are so longsuffering with non-believers, but almost merciless when one of the ministers occasionally fails us. We have become known as the army that shoots its wounded. Parents need to exercise patience with leadership in the church. Most youth leaders are not in their fifties; they are in their twenties. Give the leader space to grow in wisdom and knowledge as God does a work in them and through them. When patience is given, it will be for the glory of God and for the good of the teenager.

PROTECT SPIRITUAL LEADERSHIP

II Thessalonians 3:6 says, *"Now we command you, brethren, in the name of our Lord Jesus Christ, that ye withdraw yourselves from every brother that walketh disorderly, and not after the tradition which he received of us."* Be cautious about allowing the teenager to associate with families who are openly critical of their leaders. What may not be tolerated in your home may be practiced in someone else's. Parents and teenagers should learn not only to stand *for* leadership, but also to stand *with* leadership. Taking a verbal stand will silence the critic from getting to your teenager.

Satan has no new plan. He will usually tempt the one under authority. The very first temptation in the Bible was to get Eve out from under the authority of God and her husband. The prodigal son was tempted to get out from under the authority of his father. The devil still works the same way today. If

> The very first temptation in the Bible was to get Eve out from under the authority of God and her husband.

he can tear down the wall of spiritual leadership in the young person's life, then he has won a great victory. Work hard to keep teenagers under the spiritual authority God has placed above them.

CHAPTER 15

THE WALL OF PERSONAL SEPARATION

Personal separation is commanded in the Bible. II Corinthians 6:17 says, *"Wherefore come out from among them, and be ye separate, saith the Lord, and touch not the unclean thing; and I will receive you."* The purpose of establishing personal standards of holiness is to help teens progress toward the ultimate goal of Christlikeness in their lives.

In this matter of personal separation there are two trains of thought. First is separation *from* the world and second is separation *unto* the Lord. It is possible to be the first without being the second. The secret of separation is that being separated from the world is the *result* of separated unto the Lord. As we draw ourselves near to Christ, we will distance ourselves from the world. Our nearness to the Lord will crowd out the wrong things from our lives. This is true, biblical separation.

We find a good example of this in Luke 8:26-39, in the story of the man from Gadara. The Bible says he was bound with chains and fetters, he wore no clothes, and he dwelled in the tombs. When he met the Lord of salvation, he was delivered of the demons and his soul was set free. When the people of the city came back to see him, they found an amazing sight. The man from Gadara was **"sitting at the feet of Jesus, clothed, and in his right mind"** (Luke 8:35). Where did he learn to live by modesty and morality? The answer is obvious. The place where you will establish personal convictions and learn of separation is at the feet of Jesus Christ.

Youth leaders who preach and promote personal separation are often labeled as "legalists." This is a rabbit trail of the devil leading us off the path to personal holiness. Being a separated Christian is not *legalism*, but it is *loyalty* to Christ and His Word. Separation is not *bondage*, but it is *boundaries* in which we have freedom in Christ. Separation is not *narrowness*, but it is *nearness* to the person of Jesus Christ. Personal separation is the result of having a heart that is transformed. What is in the heart will eventually come to the surface. True separation does not work its way in from the outside; it works its way out from the inside.

> Our nearness to the Lord will crowd out the wrong things from our lives.

Teenagers need help in establishing personal convictions in their lives. Someone said that convictions are the net that keeps you from falling into sin. There are four general areas where teenagers must establish convictions that lead to separation:

THE ISSUE OF PERSONAL APPEARANCE AND DRESS

I Corinthians 11:14 says, *"Doth not even nature itself teach you, that, if a man have long hair, it is a shame unto him?"* I Timothy 2:9 says, *"In like manner also, that women adorn themselves in modest apparel, with shamefacedness and sobriety; not with broided hair, or gold, or pearls, or costly array."* God's Word teaches that there should be a distinct difference between the saved and the unsaved, especially in matters of appearance and dress. Teenagers should be instructed to avoid immodest clothing. Dressing immodestly means putting on any clothing that draws the focus of attention to the sexual zones of the body. A good motto for the Christian should be, "Dress to be admired, not desired!"

Another concern is the wearing of clothing that distracts from one's gender. It is an abomination before God when a man's masculinity or a woman's femininity is reduced by extreme measures. There should be a noticeable *difference from a*

> A good motto for the Christian should be, "Dress to be admired, not desired!"

distance. Some of the world's styles are simply unacceptable to the Christian young person seeking God's best for their lives. As the salt of the earth, we should never lose our distinctiveness. When *Hollywood* has more influence upon how we look and dress than the *Holy Word* of God, we are in serious trouble. It is vitally important that our convictions of separation are based solely upon the Bible.

THE ISSUE OF MORALITY AND PURITY

We are living in a day where teens are throwing out the window everything that is decent and moral. Personal morals of purity are considered "old-fashioned" by many young people. A recent survey of nine hundred teenagers by *Seventeen* magazine revealed:
- over 75% have used birth control.
- 37% of the girls and 58% of the boys said there is nothing wrong with premarital intercourse and said, "I intend to try it" or "I have done it."
- Only 22% of the girls and 16% of the boys said that sex before marriage was a bad idea.[17]

Unfortunately, Christian teenagers appear to be no exception. Research shows that by the twelfth grade, 62% of today's churched teens have been sexually involved.[18] God's Word gives us a message of morality.

- It is God's will that young people remain sexually inactive until they are married. I Thessalonians 4:3-4 says, *"For this is the will of God, even your sanctification, that ye should abstain from fornication: That every one of you should know how to possess his vessel in sanctification and honour."*
- God requires purity and holy living in the life of a Christian. I Thessalonians 4:7 says, *"For God hath not called us unto uncleanness, but unto holiness."*
- A life lived with no morals is headed for destruction. Proverbs 14:34 says, *"Righteousness exalteth a nation: but sin is a reproach to any people."*

THE ISSUE OF ENTERTAINMENT AND ACTIVITIES

A survey of two thousand young people in grades three through twelve revealed:

- A young person watches an average of twenty-one hours of TV each week.
- Over 58% have a TV in their bedroom.
- Offensive language and reference to homosexuality on TV has increased more than 5 ½ times in the last ten years.

- 21% look at something on the Internet that they would not want their parents to know about.[19]

- ## TV/Movies
  The greatest molding factor in the present generation has become the influence of television. One author estimates the average Christian seventeen-year-old has watched over eighteen thousand hours of TV.[20] Yet, they spend only a few hours a week at church. Over thirty percent of our homes are classified as "constant television families," meaning that the TV is never turned off during the day, even when no one is watching it. Television is becoming the babbling backdrop against which our whole lives are being lived out. Television saturates our mind with wickedness and worldliness, especially in sexual themes. Charles Hadden Spurgeon said this: "The further a man goes in lust and iniquity, the more dead he becomes to purity and holiness. He loses the power to appreciate the beauties of virtue or to be disgusted with the abominations of vice." A standard of separation can be established in the area of entertainment and activities by adhering to Psalm 101:3-7 and Lamentations 3:51.

- **Dancing**
Senior proms and school dances have only one thing wrong with them. They solicitate the lust of the flesh, the lust of the eyes, and the pride of life. Dancing stirs sexual lust in the minds of young men and women. It allows the young person to simulate sexual acts while still having their clothes on. Most teenagers do not have to be convinced that certain things are wrong. Rather they need help in overcoming their addictions to these habits of sin. Exodus 32:19 says, *"And it came to pass, as soon as he came nigh unto the camp, that he saw the calf, and the dancing: and Moses' anger waxed hot, and he cast the tables out of his hands, and brake them beneath the mount."* When the children of Egypt were in a backslidden condition, they found themselves involved in idolatry and dancing. (It is also interesting to note that John the Baptist was beheaded at a dance in the New Testament.) You will find that idol worship, the wrong kind of music, illicit sex, and dancing always go together. J. Edgar Hoover made this statement:

"Most juvenile crime has its inception in the dance hall, either public or private."

▪ **Music**

The Bible tells us in Ephesians 5:19, ***"Speaking to yourselves in psalms and hymns and spiritual songs, singing and making melody in your heart to the Lord."*** According to a Louis-Harris polling agency, 87% of all young people listen to rock and roll music. Music is an important area when it comes to standards of separation. The music we listen to has a mighty influence upon our lives, attitudes and spiritual condition.

Young people should be taught to draw their lines in the right place. There is no such thing as "gospel rock" or "contemporary Christian" music. The very names themselves are a contradiction one to another. This is like saying there is such a thing as Christian prostitution. Christians should never be identified with music that is sensual and secular.

The Bible guidelines in the previous verse promote psalms, hymns, and spiritual songs. A psalm is scripture set to music. A hymn is something that talks about and glorifies God. A spiritual song is a song of praise testifying about what God has done in a life. The Scripture teaches that music is to stay within those three categories. A Christ-honoring song will emphasize the melody above the rhythm.

- **Violent Video Games**

    Psalm 11:5 says, *"The LORD trieth the righteous: but the wicked and him that loveth violence his soul hateth."* Video games are a popular trend with today's teenager. Viewing a constant display of blood and violence will dull the senses and desensitize the human heart and mind. Teenagers should be encouraged to separate from the appearance of evil and violence.

THE ISSUE OF THE PHYSICAL BODY

The Bible says in I Corinthians 3:16-17, *"Know ye not that ye are the temple of God, and that the Spirit of God dwelleth in you? If any man defile the temple of God, him shall God destroy; for the temple of God is holy, which temple ye are.*" According to this passage, we are to bring glory to God through our body. This would indicate that gluttony, smoking, chewing, and drinking are sins against the body. Someone said that the family that prays together stays together. In the same sense, the family that smokes together chokes together. Practicing separation in our bodies would also involve body piercing and tattoos. Leviticus 19:28 condemns this popular trend today. *"Ye shall not make any cuttings in your flesh for the dead, nor print any marks upon you: I am the LORD."*

God's blueprint is very clear on most matters of personal separation. When the Bible does not name the particular sin in question, then there are ten principles that can be considered when helping the teenager establish personal convictions.

1. Does it violate a direct command of God? I John 2:3
2. Does it please God? I John 3:22
3. Will it hinder my work for God? Hebrews 12:1
4. Does it offend other Christians? I Corinthians 8:13
5. Can you thank God for it? Colossians 3:17

6. Can you do it whole heartedly as unto the Lord? Colossians 3:23
7. Is it considered worldly? I John 2:15-16
8. Is there any doubt about it? Romans 14:23
9. Does it glorify the Lord? I Corinthians 6:20
10. Do my counselors in the Lord feel that it is right for me to do? Proverbs 11:14

Personal separation is the wall of protection that God wants us to build around our lives and around our relationship with Him. God wants us to construct some high, strong walls built on Bible principles that will protect us from sin and temptation. These walls will prevent the world, the flesh, and the devil from having complete access to our lives and thoughts. When we refuse to live inside the protection of those walls, then we forfeit the protection that is provided by those walls.

Section VI

Shingling the Roof

The roof of any structure has one primary purpose: to provide shelter from the outside elements. Storms will eventually come. Rain, snow, sleet, hail, and heat will seek their entrance. A roof provides shelter from the intrusion of unwelcome weather. Shingling the roof is not an easy job, but it is a necessary job. When rafters, insulation, plywood, underlayment, and shingles are properly placed, there is a sense of completion and security to those living within.

The Biblical youth ministry must seek to protect young people from the harmful elements of life. When no shelter is provided, the teenager has no refuge from the fiery darts of the wicked one. Satan is the prince and power of the air. He is seeking an entrance into the hearts and minds of young people. It is the responsibility of the youth leader to provide a sheltered youth ministry in which teenagers can grow and mature in Christian service. This is not easy. It involves taking a strong stand against compromise, carnality, worldliness, and evil influences that seek to destroy the important work of youth ministry. There must be a frequent inspection of the roof to safeguard against cracks and leaks. If there is a crack in the roof, water will find it. Satan is busy looking for one small area in which he can infiltrate the youth ministry. May God help us to shingle the roof and provide the necessary shelter against the enemy of our souls.

CHAPTER 16

SHELTERING THE YOUTH MINISTRY FROM SATAN

II Corinthians 2:11 says, *"Lest Satan should get an advantage of us: for we are not ignorant of his devices."* There is a multiplicity of devices Satan can use to destroy youth ministries of any size. Satan's devices have never changed. The battles that teenagers faced in the Bible, are the same battles teens are facing today. The youth leader is not to be ignorant of Satan's devices. Satan will exalt the pleasures of wickedness and hide from young people the consequences. Satan knows God has a plan for the teenager's life; therefore, he employs every device to destroy the child of God, especially teenagers. J.C. Ryle says this about teenagers, "You are those on whom he displays all his choicest temptations. He spreads the net with the most watchful carefulness, to entangle your hearts. He baits his traps with the sweetest morsels, to get you into his power. He displays his merchandise before your eyes with his utmost ingenuity, in order to make you buy his sugared poisons, and eat his

> The youth leader is not to be ignorant of Satan's devices.

accursed dainties. You are the grand object of his attack. May the Lord rebuke him, and deliver you out of his hands."[21]

In Daniel chapter 1:1, we find a young man named Daniel, who was targeted by the devil. ***"In the third year of the reign of Jehoiakim king of Judah came Nebuchadnezzar king of Babylon unto Jerusalem, and beseiged it."***

> This is what contemporary Christian or gospel rock attempts to do. It mixes the message of God with the music of the devil.

Nebuchadnezzar is a type of the devil. Satan has no new plan, just an old plan with a new disguise. To accomplish his purpose, he sought after and took captive those young people of the "kings seed". He wanted the "cream of the crop". Those with *Integrity* ***"...Children in whom is no blemish..."***, those with *Intellect* ***"...skillful in all wisdom, and cunning in knowledge, and understanding science..."***, and those with *Influence* ***"...and such as had ability in them to stand in the king's palace..."*** (Daniel 1:4) The more you mean to God, the more Satan will come after your life and Influence. There are several specific areas where Daniel fell under the attack of Satan.

THE ATTACK UPON HIS FAMILY

The Bible indicates that Daniel was part of a royal family. The plan was to remove or separate Daniel from his family back in Jerusalem. Daniel 1:3 says, ***"And the king spake unto Ashpenaz the master of his eunuchs, that he should bring certain of the children of Israel and of the king's seed, and of the princes."*** Satan's desire was to bring him under the influence of Babylonian captivity. He wanted Daniel to forget about his heritage and to forsake the God of his parents. Satan's desire today is to remove young people from the guidance, protection, and authority of the home. Satan is the master of division. He divided the Prodigal Son from his home, he divided Daniel from his home, and he will cause division in our homes if we are not careful. If he can cause young people to rebel against the authority of the parent, then he can cause them to rebel against the authority of God. There is no exception to the rule. The local church youth ministry must recognize Satan's goal and seek to strengthen the families in our church.

THE ATTACK UPON HIS FUTURE

Nebuchadnezzar's desire was to build his own kingdom. To rule the world, he had to make Chaldeans out of the children of God. Daniel 1:4 says, ***"...and whom*** *they might teach the learning and the tongue of the Chaldeans.*" He wanted to change their culture and the way they thought by giving them new names that identified them with Babylon's idols. (Daniel 1:5-7) Remember when God delivered the children of Israel? Satan knew he couldn't put God's people back into Egypt, so he put Egypt back into the hearts of God's people. When you compromise in the *present*, it will change the *future*. The attack today is upon the future of God's young people. Satan doesn't want teenagers to think like a Christian nor does he want them to be identified with a Christian heritage. He wants God's people to adopt strange names, strange culture, strange thinking, and strange music.

Satan knows the powerful grip that music can have on a young person's life. Young people make heroes out of ungodly entertainers and allow them to influence their minds. Rock music, from its very inception, has always been anti-God, anti-morality, and anti-parent. It is a promoter of rebellion, sex, suicide, drugs, and violence.

Newsweek estimated that from the seventh to twelfth grade, teens will listen to over eleven thousand hours of rock videos, tapes, and CD's. The survey found that teens listen to the radio an average of fourteen hours a week, and to rock music a total of twenty-eight hours a week.[22] The wrong kind of music can be one of Satan's greatest devices because it is a tremendous stimulator of evil thoughts and immorality. Even contemporary Christian music is a device of the devil. Romans 1:18 says, **"...who hold the truth in unrighteousness."** This is what contemporary Christian or gospel rock attempts to do. It brings truth and unrighteousness together. It mixes the *message of God* with the *music of the devil.* There should always be a wide difference between God's music and the devil's music. Contemporary Christian music tries to bridge the gap between the two. The word contemporary means *"to be in step with the world."* The word Christianity means *"to be in step with Christ."* You cannot be in step with the world and in step with

> Settling for second best is a common pitfall of many teenagers.

Christ at the same time. Satan uses this type of music to mix that which is fleshly with that which is holy in an effort to make it palatable for the child of God. The word "contemporary" and the word "Christian" do not belong in the same sentence. The local church youth ministry should encourage teenagers to proudly indentify with genuine, Biblical Christianity. May we teach young people to remember their heritage and never "sell out" the future upon the altar of the present.

THE ATTACK UPON HIS FLESH

The prince of the eunuchs designed a special diet to be eaten which gave no regard for the Law of God nor convictions of Daniel. This violated the conscience of Daniel. If he would have partaken, he would have defiled himself. Daniel 1:8 says, ***"...But Daniel purposed in his heart that he would not defile himself with the portion of the king's meat, nor with the wine which he drank: therefore he requested of the prince of the eunuchs that he might not defile himself."*** Victory over the flesh began in the heart of Daniel. Notice that long before the moment of temptation came, Daniel decided in his heart that was going to please the Lord. If there was a person who could have justified a reason to please his flesh, it was Daniel. He was 700 miles away from home, away from the supervision of his parents, and away from the environment of Jerusalem. Nebuchadnezzar set the table with a royal provision that was hard to refuse. But Daniel decided, "I'm going to live the Jerusalem way while I'm in Babylon!" His convictions proved ten times better than any compromise the world had to offer. (Daniel 1:20)

The hardest battle that teenagers are fighting today is against their own fleshly desires. As youth leaders, we must be bold to tell young people that God's way may not be popular, but it is always better in the end. The path of holiness may not be well traveled, but the end leads to life everlasting!

THE ATTACK UPON HIS FAITH

In Daniel 6:20, Darius posed a question that was a subtle attack upon Daniel's faith. ***"...is thy God, whom thou servest contiually, able to deliver thee from the lions ?"*** Satan's subtle desire is to destroy any measure of faith that young people have in God. He wants them to doubt the abilty of God in their moment of crisis. This troubled generation needs to know there is a God in Heaven who is still able to deliver when they reach the lions den or the fiery furnace. We need not to quench any measure of faith in God. Our youth ministries must cultivate young people with great faith in God, who ***"..believe that He is, and that He is a rewarder of them that diligently seek Him."*** (Hebrews 11:7)

The battle still rages today. Satan has not altered his attack. The local church must provide a sheltering ministry for teenagers. A refuge that will *safegaurd* their family, *stir* their faith, *stand* against their flesh, and *strengthen* their future in the Lord. ***"In the fear of the Lord is strong confidence: and His children shall have a place of refuge."*** (Proverbs 14:26)

CHAPTER 17

SHELTERING THE YOUTH MINISTRY FROM THE SCORNER

"How long, ye simple ones, will ye love simplicity? And the scorners delight in their scorning, and fools hate knowledge?" (Proverbs 1:22). This verse speaks of three groups of people: the simple, the fool, and the scorner. You will find all three of these groups of people in every youth ministry.

The *fool*, according to the Bible, is someone that has no heart-knowledge of Jesus Christ. Psalm 53:1 says, *"The fool hath said in his heart, There is no God..."* The Bible says in Romans 10:10, *"For with the heart man believeth unto...salvation."* When a person rejects Christ in his heart, he is foolish. It is a fool who comes face to face with God and does not believe in his own heart the message of salvation.

The *simple* are those whom God takes and makes wise. Psalm 119:130 says, *"The entrance of thy words giveth light; it giveth understanding unto the simple."* Proverbs 14:15 describes the simple as those who *"believeth every word."* In other words, the simple man receives the Word of God and the instruction from God's servant with an open heart and mind. The simple are tenderhearted and sensitive to the Holy Spirit. We are instructed in Psalm 19:7 to make *"wise the simple."* In the average youth group, the majority will consist of those who are simple. Our responsibility is to protect the simple and make them wise. Satan will attack the youth ministry by coming after the simple. He uses the scorner to accomplish his destructive desires. The Bible says in Proverbs 1:32, *"For the turning away of the simple shall slay them..."*

The word *scorn* or *scorning* is found 27 times in the Word of God. The scornful teenager has the potential to destroy the spirit and influence of the youth ministry. We must realize that the simple will not make spiritual decisions until we are willing to deal with the scorner.

DETECTING THE SCORNER

1. The Scorner's Disguise
- He is filled with pride (Proverbs 21:24).
- He is a carnal Christian who portrays himself as spiritual (II Timothy 3:5).
- He does most of his work behind the scenes (Psalm 22:7-8).

2. The Scorner's Dialogue
- He mocks those who are doing right (Job 12:4).
- He criticizes the work of the Lord (Nehemiah 2:19).
- He speaks out against spiritual leadership in public or private.

3. The Scorner's Disposition
- He delights in causing trouble (Proverbs 1:22).
- He hates to be reproved or corrected (Proverbs 9:8, 13:1).
- He has a sarcastic attitude toward spiritual things.

4. The Scorner's Domination
- He struggles to turn the heart of the simple away from God (Proverbs 1:32).
- He sets himself up in competition against the spiritual leader.

5. The Scorner's Damage
- He robs the spiritual leader of his influence upon others, rendering him ineffective.
- The spiritual leader will pay a price when confronting the scorner (Proverbs 9:7).

6. The Scorner's Destruction

- He will not seek wisdom from the spiritual leader (Proverbs 15:12).
- He will reap what he sows (Proverbs 1:29-32).

DISCIPLINING THE SCORNER

There are four necessary and Biblical steps we must take when disciplining the scorner:

1. Smite the Scorner

Proverbs 19:25 says, ***"Smite a scorner, and the simple will beware: and reprove one that hath understanding, and he will understand knowledge."*** To *smite* the scorner does not mean to strike them; it means "to bring them low." They must be repremanded in a stern but loving way. Have an appointment with them. Tell them how they are hurting people and that you are aware of their scorning. Speak to their parents about their actions and attitudes. Warn them privately and pray with them. In this stage, there is still hope that the scorner will hear instruction and line up with leadership.

2. Punish the Scorner

Proverbs 21:11 says, ***"When the scorner is punished, the simple is made wise: and when the wise is instructed, he receiveth knowledge."*** If step one does not work, the next step is to *punish* the scorner. This means "to openly rebuke them." Everyone needs to know that the scorner is being dealt with. Do not honor them or let them lead in anything. If they are non-verbal in rebellion, sit them away from others. Ask them to sit with their parents in Sunday school and church for a period of time. This type of discipline teaches other teenagers that it is a privilege to be in the youth ministry.

3. Cast Out the Scorner

Proverbs 22:10 says, ***"Cast out the scorner, and contention shall go out; yea, strife and reproach shall cease."*** After the scorner has been warned and punished, the third step is to *cast out* the scorner. This is always a tough decision that should ultimately be made by the pastor. The Lord Jesus chose to cast out the scorner before He raised the damsel from the dead. (Mark 5:40) The teen is not cast out of the church, but they are cast out of the youth ministry until they experience a personal revival for all to see. They are out of youth activities, out of teen soul winning, out of teen trips, and out of Christian service. A scornful teenager who has reached this level of discipline, should not be allowed back into the youth group until a genuine act of repentance is noticed by the Pastor and youth leader. When the Word of God is followed, a good spirit will return to the youth ministry. Spiritual decisions will be made again. Contention, strife, and reproach will end when the scorner is cast out.

4. Turn the Scorner Over to God's Hand for Judgment

Proverbs 19:29 says, *"Judgments are prepared for scorners, and stripes for the back of fools."* At this point, only God can turn around the scorner. If they are not brought to this point, there can be no real help. God uses judgment to turn the scorner back to Him.

The wise youth leader will provide a shelter of protection from Satan and any scornful influence upon the youth ministry.

PHASE VII

SURVIVING THE FINAL INSPECTION

The last stage of every construction project is to pass the test of a final inspection. Every detail of labor will be examined by the careful eye of the inspector. Our work must have his approval. Successful achievement is not determined by the builder, it is determined by the inspector alone. A sense of genuine fulfillment comes when his commendation is awarded.

The Bible teaches that one day our labor in the Lord's work will end. Jesus said in John 9:4, *"I must work the works of him that sent me, while it is day: the night cometh, when no man can work."* Our labor in the youth ministry must be done urgently, effectively, efficiently, and soberly in the light of eternity. When the day of the Lord appears, every Christian worker will give an account at the Judgment Seat of Christ.

The apostle Paul gave twice to Timothy the special instruction to *"lay hold on eternal life"* (I Timothy 6:12, 19). This does not teach that eternity can be *purchased,* it teaches that eternity should be *pondered.* All Christian service should be done with eternity in view. No Christian will be exempt from this day of final inspection. Our ultimate reward is to hear the Chief Inspector say, ***"Well done, thou good and faithful servant."***

CHAPTER 18

THE ETERNAL MEASURE OF THE YOUTH MINISTRY

It is a sobering thought to know that eternity will shed light on our labor in the youth ministry. All spiritual work will be measured at the Judgment Seat of Christ. As a youth minister for more than 18 years, there have been times when I have felt like a complete failure with young people. There have also been times where I have felt accomplished in working with teenagers. True success in youth work is not determined by feelings. It is measured by our faithfulness to the Word of God and our obedience to His will for our lives. If we expect to receive a reward for our work in the youth ministry, then we must make certain that we have accomplished the right goals.

As we examine the overall picture, there are several indicators that will determine if true success has been achieved. A youth leader can check his success in youth ministry by honestly answering the following questions.

All spiritual work will be measured at the Judgment Seat of Christ.

A YOUTH WORKERS CHECKLIST

1. Have I *earnestly* sought to obey the Great Commission?

> It is impossible to neglect the Great Commission and consider our youth ministry a success.

Matthew 28:19-20 says, *"Go ye therefore and teach all nations, baptizing them in the name of the Father, and of the Son, and of the Holy Ghost: Teaching them to observe all things I have commanded you..."* It is impossible to neglect the Great Commission and consider our youth ministry a success. Reaching the lost for Christ and discipling them in the faith should always be on the front burner in our thinking. There are so many rabbit-trail substitutes that would take us away from accomplishing the most important goal. A successful youth minister will be a soul winner, and he will teach young people to win souls. The Great Commission must be understood and obeyed. It is broken down into four parts. We must go, explain salvation, baptize, and then teach all things. This is God's blueprint for all people. There is a divine order that should be followed and never changed. To *go* means that I have given time each week to share the gospel with lost young people, taking advantage of every opportunity to be a witness for Christ. To *teach* means that I have explained the way of salvation in a clear and consistent manner. I have not frustrated the gospel message. To *baptize* means that I have encouraged those to take the next step after salvation, identifying with the death, burial, and resurrection of Christ. To *teach all things* means I have helped young people to grow in their faith both spiritually, mentally, and socially.

2. Have I *encouraged* the relationship between the Teenager and the Parent?

Colossians 3:20-21 says, *"Children, obey your parents in all things: for this is well pleasing unto the Lord. Fathers, provoke not your children to anger, lest they be discouraged."* A key principle in youth ministry is to remember that the ultimate responsibility of the teenager belongs to the parent. The local church must strive to help parents perform their God-ordained role of building a unified, Christ-honoring home. The institution of the biblical home will influence the teenager far beyond their teen years. This is why the youth ministry must be a family ministry. There are many ways in which we can accomplish this goal.

- Seek to win every family member to Christ.
- Turn the hearts of young people to the authority of the parents.

- Involve parents in the youth ministry.
- Keep an open line of communication with the parent.
- Alert parents of the harmful sins that are destroying this generation of teenagers.
- Provide materials that encourage family devotional time.
- Promote books and tapes that will strengthen the parent.
- Never criticize the parent to the teenager.
- Inform the parent when counseling their teenager or when their child has made any spiritual decision.
- Plan an occasional meeting with all parents to share helpful information, encouragement, and training.
- Never plan youth activities that would interfere with important family holidays (Thanksgiving, Christmas, etc.).

An indication of true success is when you have strengthened the parent/teen relationship in the home.

3. Have I *endeared* the teenager to the ministry of the local church?

Acts 9:26-27 says, *"And when Saul was come to Jerusalem, he assayed to join himself to the disciples: but they were all afraid of him and believed not that he was a disciple. But Barnabas took him to the disciples..."* The apostle Paul turned out ot be one of the greatest Christians in the New Testament. This happened because early in his Christian life, Barnabas joined him to the fellowship of the local church. Teenagers need to be connected to the heart and ministry of the local church. This is important because the church will seek to minister to them well beyond the teen years. Why do Christian teenagers graduate from high school and appear to drop off the scene? Could it be that they were

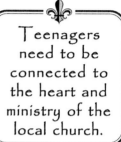

Teenagers need to be connected to the heart and ministry of the local church.

drawn to an individual and not to the institution of the local church? When our programs isolate the teenager from the parent, pastor, and church, we have done a terrible injustice. Our churches should be filled with former teenagers who are now faithful adults serving the Lord and accomplishing the will of God. When young people leave the youth ministry, they should hold the local church in high regard.

4. Have I *emphasized* the right things with teenagers?

Philippians 1:10 says, ***"That ye may approve things that are excellent: that ye may be sincere and without offence till the day of Christ."*** It is vitally important to place the emphasis in our ministry where God places the empahsis in His Word. The blessing of

God will come when the youth leader makes a deliberate decision to emphasize those things that are excellent and right. When we stand at the Judgment Seat of Christ, the foundation that we have built upon will be under review (I Corinthians 3:11-15). We must avoid the wood, hay and stubble in our ministry. So many times we create much fluff that will never stand the test of eternal fire. Fire reveals quality, not quantity. When the fire is applied to our spiritual work, only that which is essential will remain and be rewarded. We must discover from the pages of Scripture those things that are important to God. God's priority should always be our top priority. Most youth programs place an over-emphasis upon fun, fellowship, food, facilities, and the latest fads of the day. A true measure of a successful youth ministry is a recognizable emphasis upon soul winning, Bible doctrine, Scripture memory, missions, full-time service, and biblical standards. The spiritual should always supercede the secular without neglecting the joy of the Christian life.

> Fire reveals quality, not quantity.

5. Have I *engaged* young people to reach their generation for Christ?

Psalms 145:4 says, *"One generation shall praise thy works to another, and shall dclare thy mighty acts."* A prominent criterion of success is when teenagers began to reach and impact others with their life. There should be no "dead end" in the local church youth ministry. The buck does not stop at the end of the 12th grade. Teens should face an open door to serve their generation and the next for Christ! Biblical Christianity must always be passed on to those who follow us. This happens when young people have been trained and developed for spiritual leadership. The proof of successful youth ministry is not in what the leader has done, but in what his products are doing. Too often we observe young people who seem to have no burden for their generation. We must challenge them to put into practice those principles they have learned in the classroom of the local church. II Timothy 2:2 reveals a biblical way in which we can truly impact the future. ***"And the things that thou hast heard of me among many witnesses, the same commit thou to faithful men, who shall be able to teach others also."***

6. Have I *equipped* young people to enter the full-time ministry ?

Isaiah 6:8 says, ***"Also I heard the voice of the Lord, saying, Whom shall I send, and who will go for us? Then said I, Here am I; send me."*** The law of the harvest teaches us that out of every good tree will come forth good fruit. This may not happen over night, but it will eventually happen. The choicest fruit of the youth ministry are those young people who have answered the call of God and are sent forth into the work of the Lord. As a result of our labor, there should be examples of those who are serving Christ in a full-time way with their lives. A good youth ministry will make much of the need for labourers in the Lord's work. Teenagers need to see the joy of serving Jesus! We need to point out the great heroes of the faith who have given their energy for the cause of Christ. We need to promote Bible colleges to our young people. An environment must be created in the local church youth ministry that is condusive to young people serving the Lord.

> Teenagers need to see the joy of serving Jesus!

In the sport of baseball, the farm league plays a major role in the future of baseball. Their purpose is to train, develop, and equip those players to step up to the next level of major league baseball. The local church youth is the training ground where young people should be developed and promoted up to the highest level of Christian service and influence. I rejoice to see that in our local church, the Lord has sent forth those who are now pastors, missionaries, youth directors, bus and children directors, music ministers, church planters, and Christian school teachers.

The latest youth ministry trends will come and go. This checklist should help us to evaluate our present position, and it will keep us on the right course in the local church youth ministry.

CONCLUSION

The construction of a biblical youth ministry begins in the heart of the local church and it ends up at the Judgment Seat of Christ. Somewhere between the two, we are commanded to labor faithfully until the return of the Lord. Jesus said **"...I have finished the work which thou gavest me to do."** (John 17:4) It is important for us to finish what we have started in the area of youth ministry.

Have you ever noticed an abandoned building on the side of the road? There is one such building in our city. One day the ground was broken, the foundation was poured, the steel frame was erected, and the roof was added. Then suddenly, construction stopped. For some unknown reason the project was left unfinished. The building was abandoned. There are no more laborers, no more work, and no more progress. Busy hands have now become idle, and what *could* have been, will never be. This tragic story could be repeated all across America in the area of youth ministry.

This is a time when youth leaders and workers must commit ourselves, with all diligence, to finish the work God has given us to do. These can be days of great purpose and accomplishment. May we never be guilty of abandoning the teenager in their brief moment of construction. May we never abandon the youth ministry when difficulties and criticisms come our way. In Nehemiah 4:6, the Bible says, *"the people had a mind to work."* The outcome of such determination was rewarded in Nehemiah 6:15, *"So the wall was finished."* The character of our heart is not seen by what it takes to get us started, it is seen by what it takes to stop us.

I am serving the Lord today because someone took the time to build a biblical youth ministry in the heart of my local church. Faithful men and women invested in my life at every stage of construction. Foundations were laid, walls were built, protection was put in place, someone followed the blueprint, someone did not quit, someone built a youth ministry that glorified the Lord and produced something great in my life and in the lives of hundreds of others who passed along behind me.

In these last days, let us determine to construct biblical youth ministries that make a lasting difference in the lives of young people. It can still be done for the glory of God!

END NOTES

1. David C. Gibbs, Jr., *The Legal Alert*, Christian Law Association, Seminole, FL, 2000, p. 6.

2. Jack Hyles, *Teaching on Preaching*, Hyles Anderson Publications, Hammond, IN, 1996, p. 147.

3. *Webster's Dictionary*, Trident Press International, 2000 Edition, p. 108.

4. *The Visitor Pulpit Helps*, January 1997, USA Issue, Today via.

5. Jerry Ross, *The Teenager Years of Jesus Christ*, Ultimate Goal Publications, Jasonville, IN, 1999, p. 14.

6. *Newsweek*, "*Teen Religion in America*", May 2000, p. 24.

7. Mike Huckabee and George Grant, *Kid Who Kill,* Broadman and Holman Publishers, Nashville, TN, 1998, p. 72.

8. Ibid, p. 81.

9. *Newsweek*, p. 53.

10. *News-Press*, January 16, 2005, Lee County, Florida, p. 17.

11. John W. Whitehead, *Your Rights in the Public School,* The Rutherford Institute, Charlottesville, VA, 1990, p. 7.

12. Clarence Sexton, *Teens For Christ Program,* Crown Publications, Powell, TN, 1998.

13. Robert Laurent, *Keeping Your Teen In Touch With God*, David C. Cook Publishers, Elgin, IL, 1988, pp. 73-74.

14. Webster's Dictionary, p. 377.

15. Author D. Burcham, *Reaching and Teaching Through Vacation Bible School,* Convention Press, Nashville, TN, 1984, p. 7.

16. Robert Laurent, p. 12.

17. *Seventeen Magazine*, Nashville, TN, November 1, 1987, p. 1.

18. Josh McDowell, *Network News,* 1997, p.8.

19. *Newsweek*, p. 24.

20. Robert Laurent, p. 37.

21. J.C. Ryle, *Thoughts for Young Men,* Calvary Press, Amityville, NY, 1996, p. 14.

22. Walter, Trudy, and Gilbert Fremont, *Forming A New Generation*, Bob Jones University Press, Greenville, SC, 1990, p. 101.

ABOUT THE AUTHOR

Rev. Tim Hawkins was born and raised in Augusta, Georgia. He accepted Christ as Savior at the age of fifteen and surrendered to preach the gospel shortly after his conversion. He earned a Bachelors degree from Victory Baptist College of North Augusta, South Carolina in 1988, and a Masters degree from Louisiana Baptist University and Seminary in Shreveport, Louisiana in 2001.

For the past fourteen years, Tim has served as the Associate Pastor of the Gulf Coast Baptist Church in Cape Coral, Florida with Dr. Tom Sexton, Pastor. He is the founder of the *Teen Life Leadership* program and the *Baptist Youth Soul-winning* program. He serves as the Director of the *Southwest Florida Teen Conference.* Tim is a frequent speaker at churches, camps, revivals, chapel services, and teen conferences.

Rev. Hawkins and his wife, Mandy, have been married for 16 years. The Lord has blessed their home with two children – Justin Timothy and Rachel Nicole. The Hawkins family presently resides in North Fort Myers, Florida.